Color By Number Adult Coloring Book

This Color By Number book belongs to:

_____

Copyright © 2020 Color By Number Coloring Books

1. Red
2. Black
3. Green
4. Blue
5. Orange
6. Pink
7. Brown
8. Purple
9. Dark Green
10. Light Green
11. Light Blue
12. Gold
13. Violet
14. Yellow

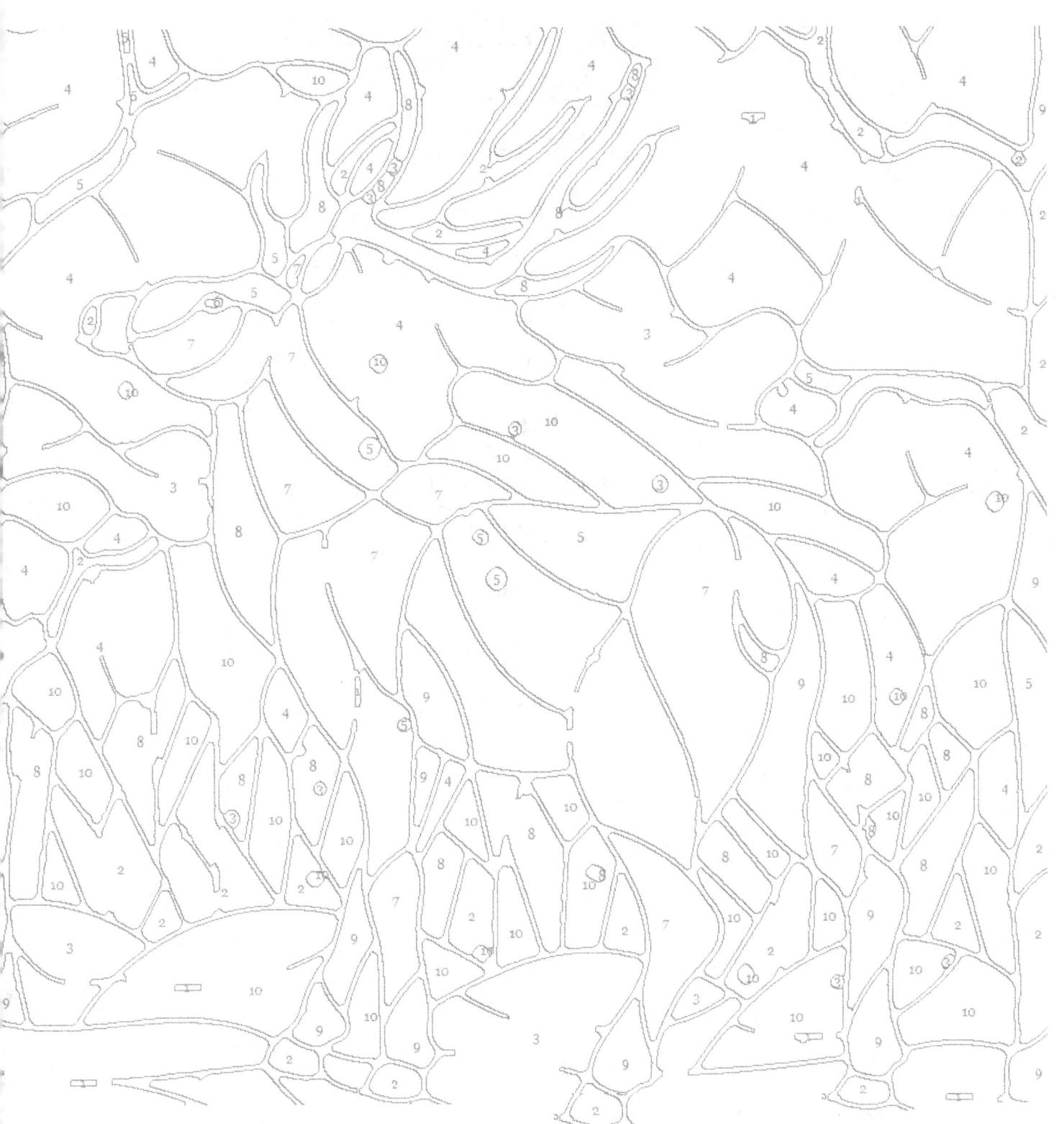

1. Blue
2. Black
3. Green
4. Red
5. Orange
6. Pink
7. Brown
8. Purple
9. Dark Green
10. Light Green
11. Light Blue
12. Gold
13. Violet
14. Yellow

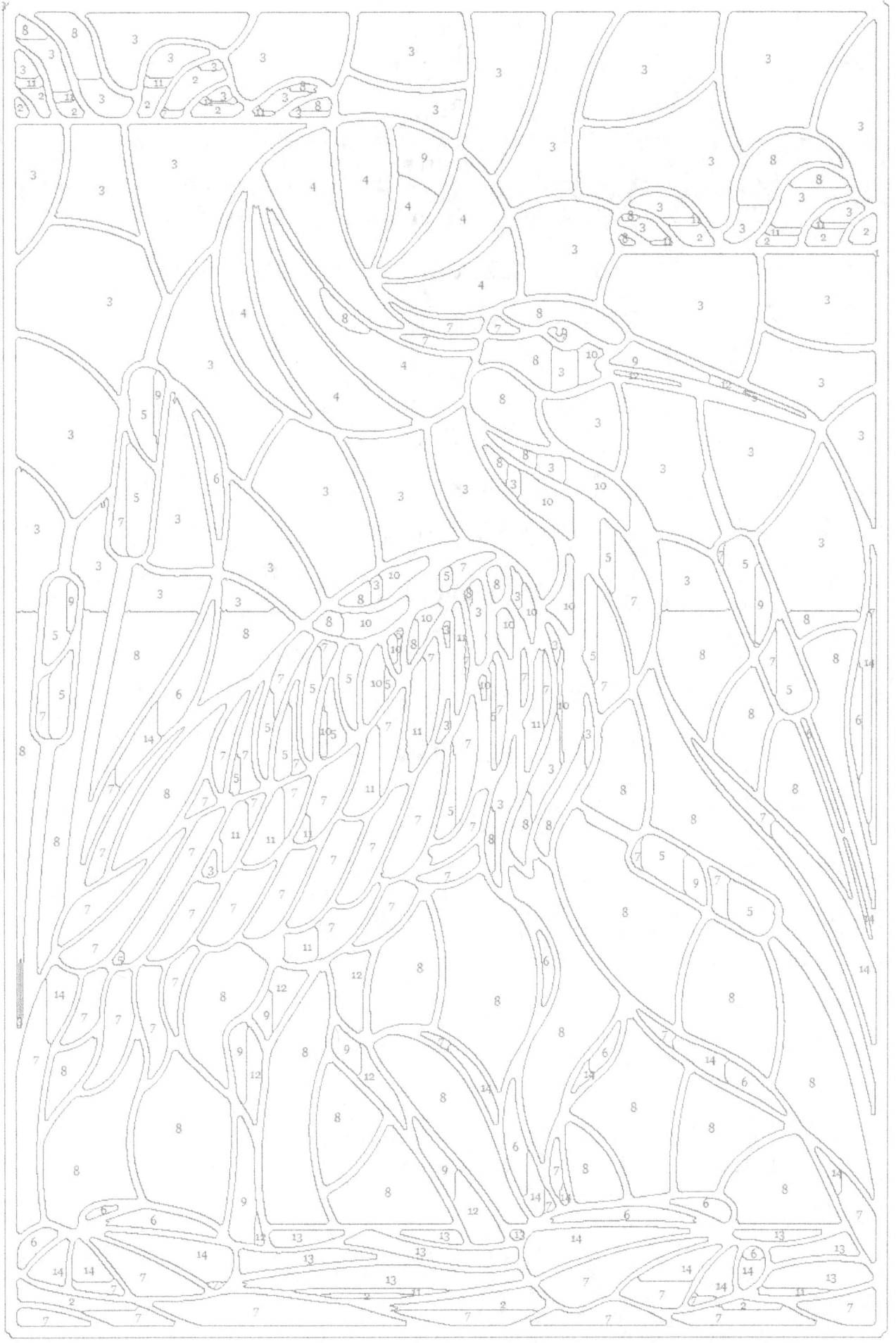

1. Black
2. Blue
3. Brown
4. Green
5. Purple
6. Pink
7. Red
8. Orange
9. Dark Green
10. Light Green
11. Light Blue
12. Gold
13. Violet
14. Yellow

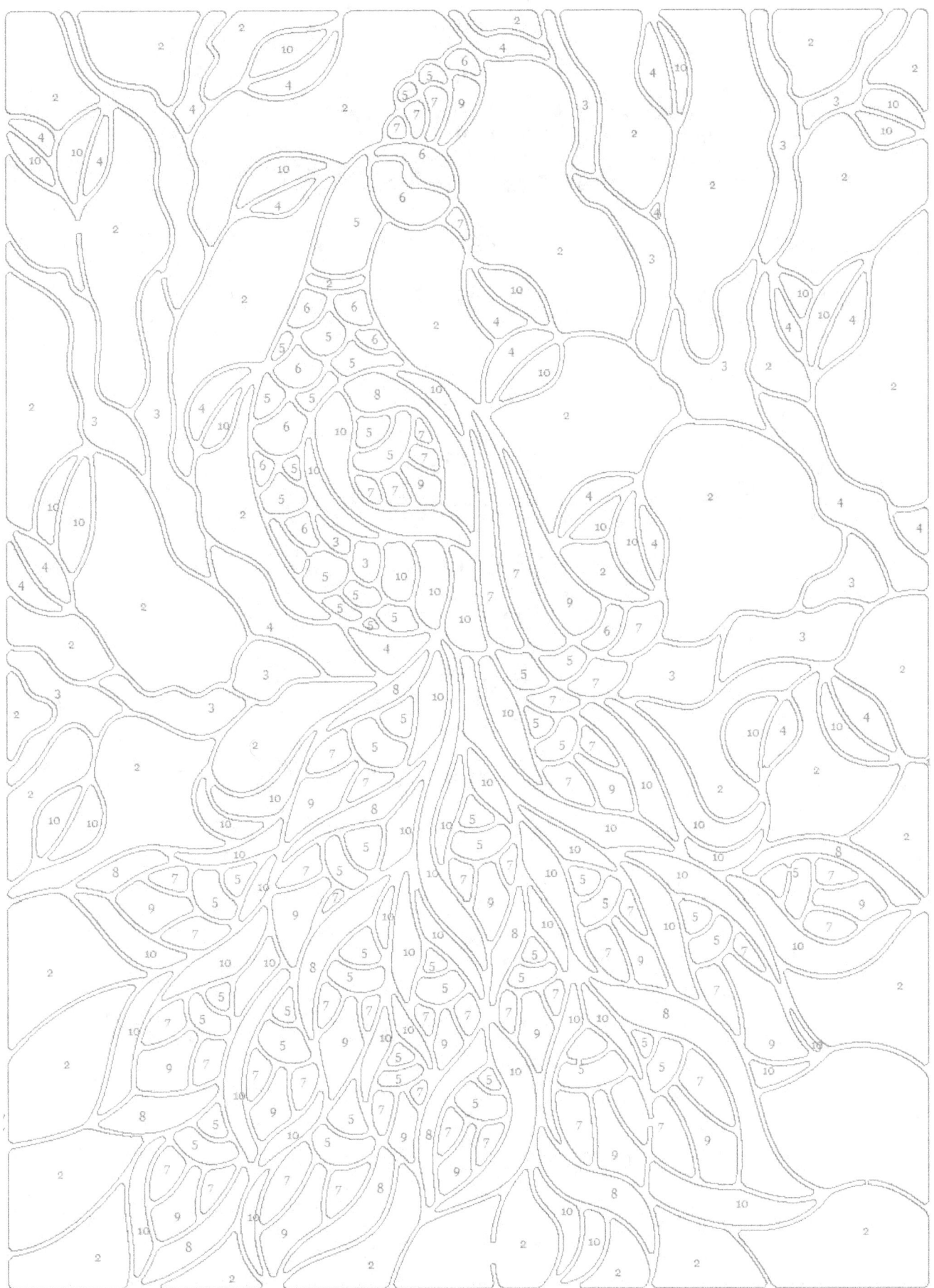

1. Pink
2. Blue
3. Yellow
4. Green
5. Purple
6. Black
7. Red
8. Dark Green
9. Orange
10. Light Green
11. Light Blue
12. Gold
13. Violet
14. Brown

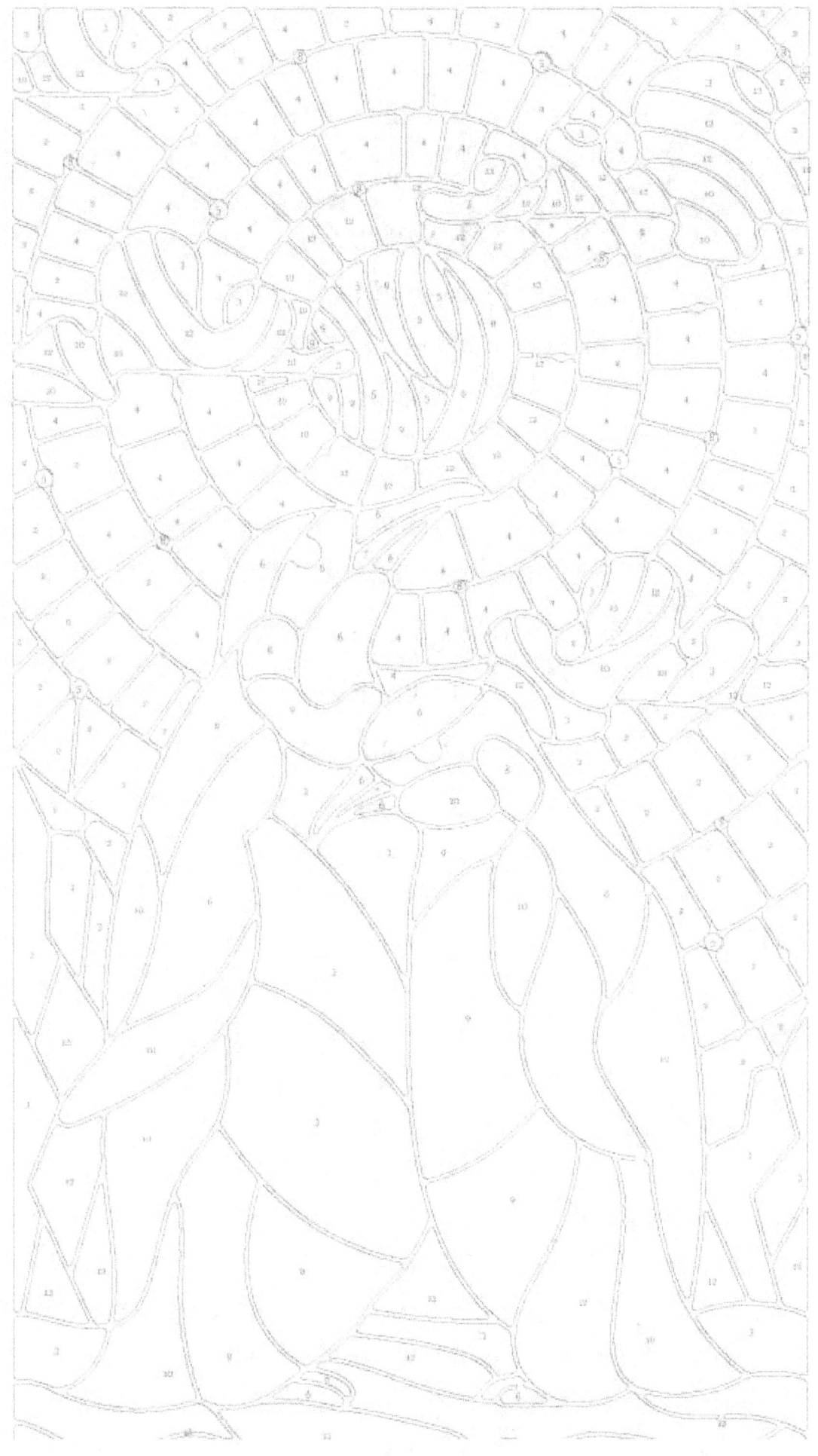

1. Blue
2. Black
3. Green
4. Red
5. Orange
6. Pink
7. Brown
8. Purple
9. Dark Green
10. Light Green
11. Light Blue
12. Gold
13. Violet
14. Yellow

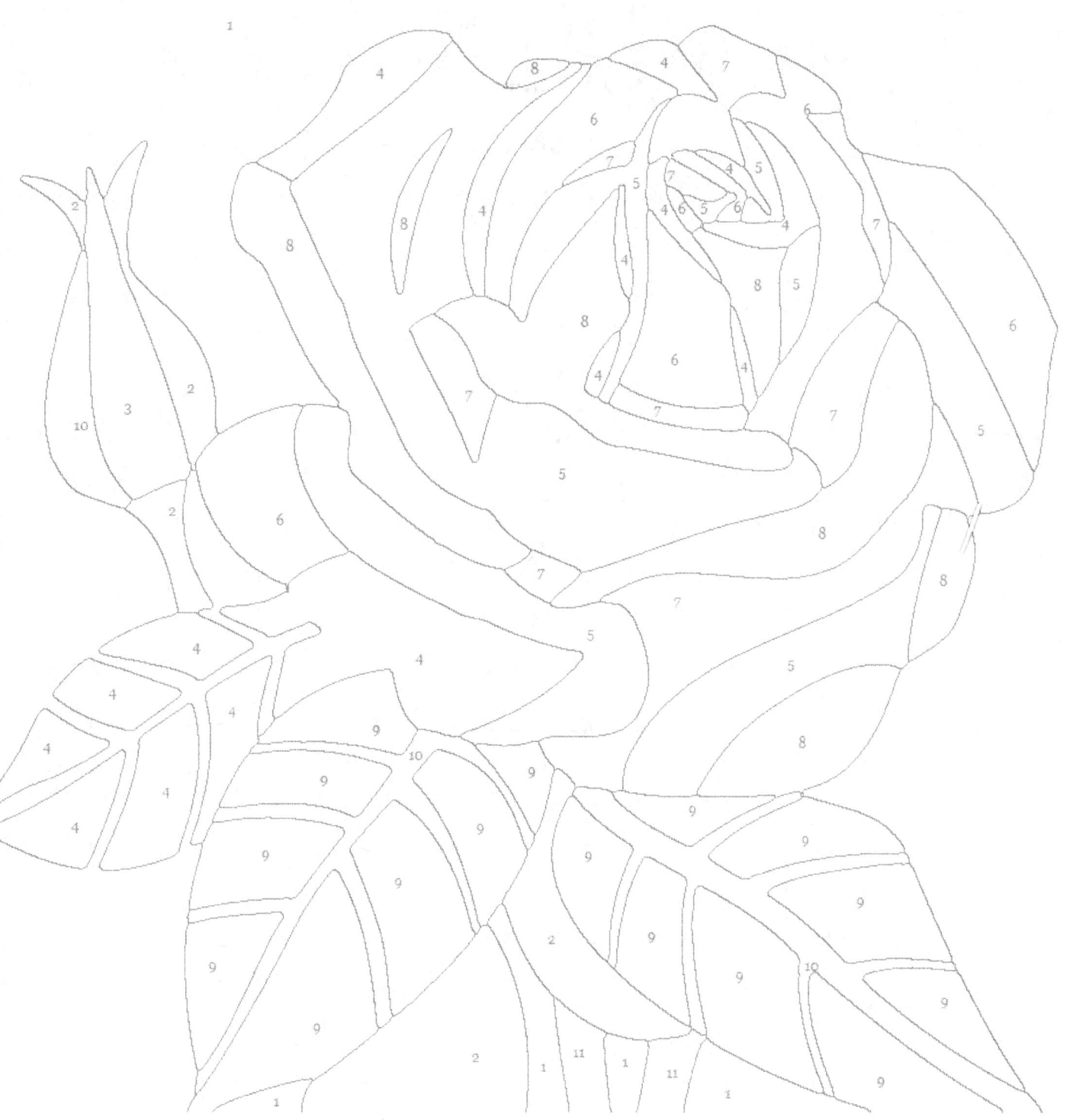

1. Blue
2. Light Green
3. Green
4. Brown
5. Red
6. Pink
7. Orange
8. Purple
9. Dark Green
10. Light Blue
11. Black
12. Gold
13. Violet
14. Yellow

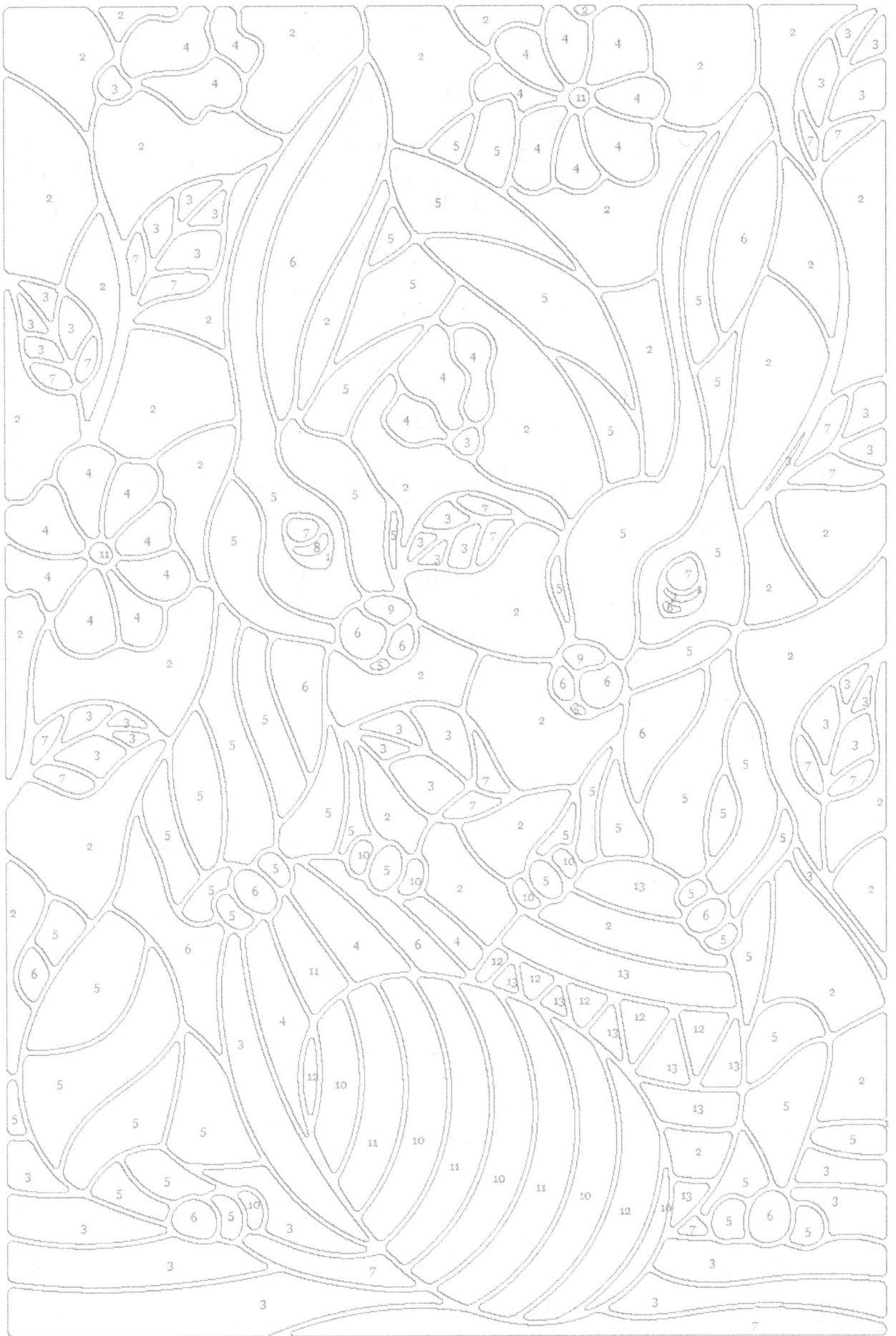

1. Blue
2. Light Green
3. Green
4. Brown
5. Red
6. Pink
7. Orange
8. Purple
9. Dark Green
10. Light Blue
11. Black
12. Gold
13. Violet
14. Yellow

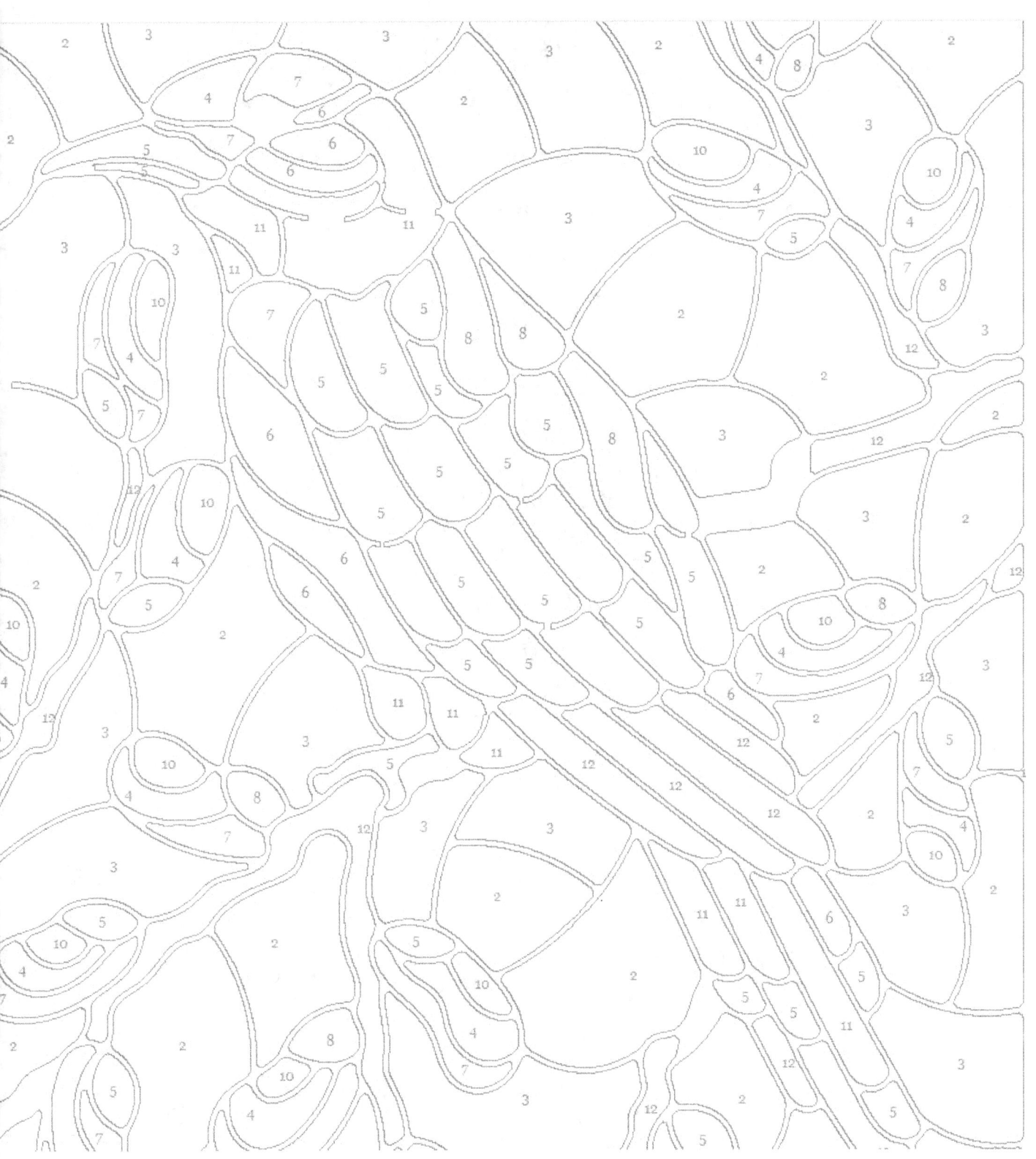

1. Blue
2. Light Green
3. Green
4. Brown
5. Red
6. Pink
7. Orange
8. Purple
9. Dark Green
10. Light Blue
11. Black
12. Gold
13. Violet
14. Yellow

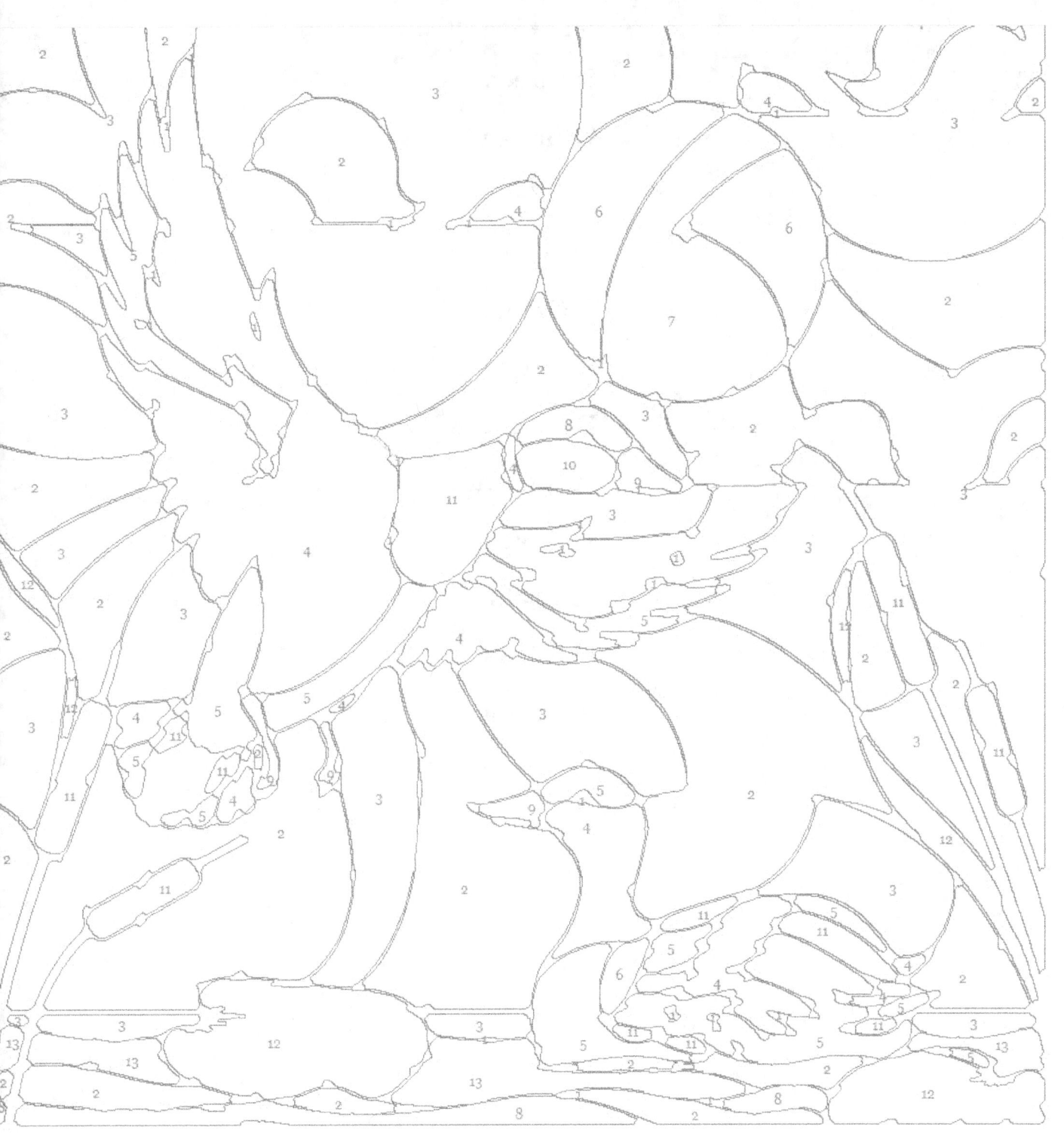

1. Blue
2. Light Green
3. Green
4. Brown
5. Red
6. Pink
7. Orange
8. Purple
9. Dark Green
10. Light Blue
11. Black
12. Gold
13. Violet
14. Yellow

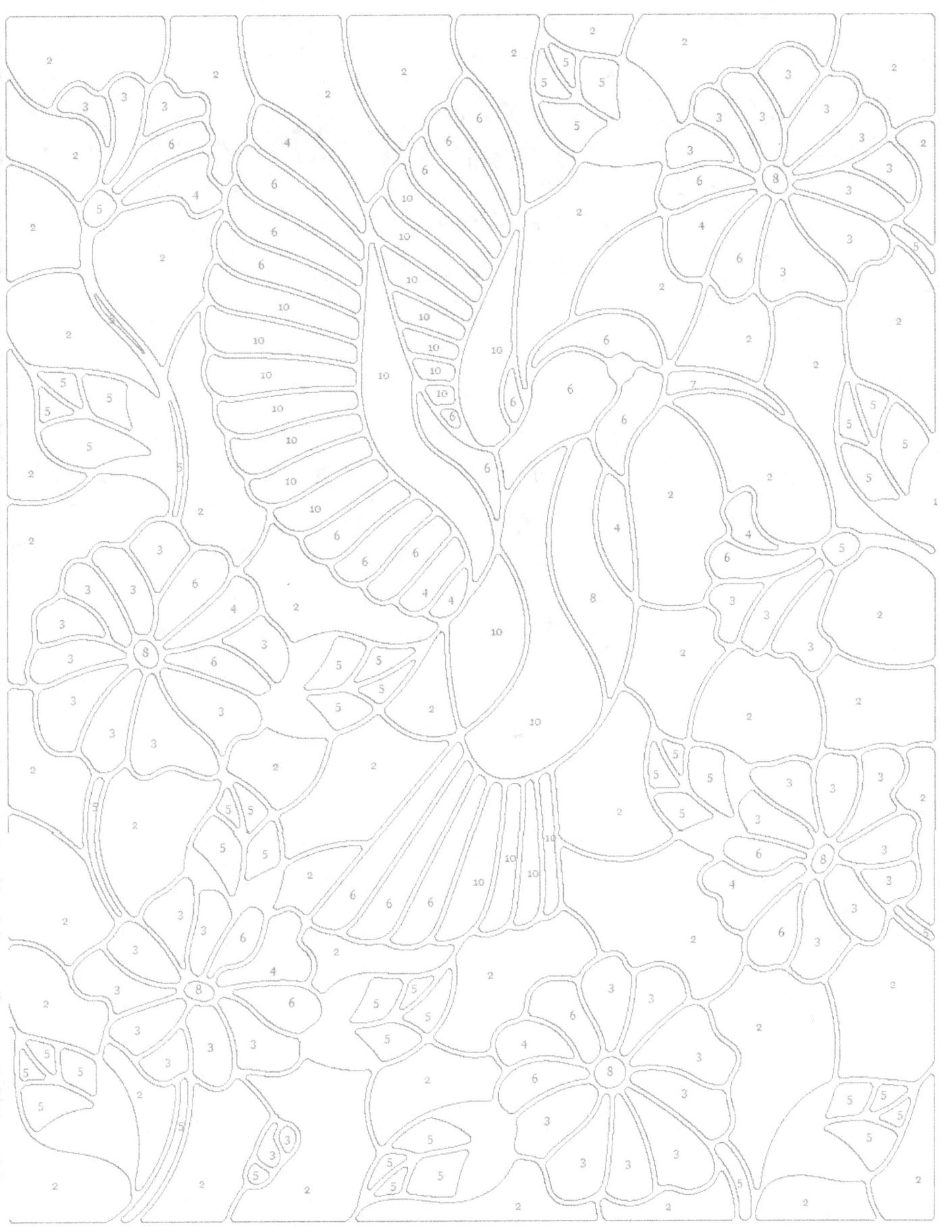

1. Red
2. Pink
3. Blue
4. Green
5. Purple
6. Light Blue
7. Light Green
8. Orange
9. Dark Red
10. Brown
11. Black
12. Dark Green
13. Gold
14. Violet
15. Yellow

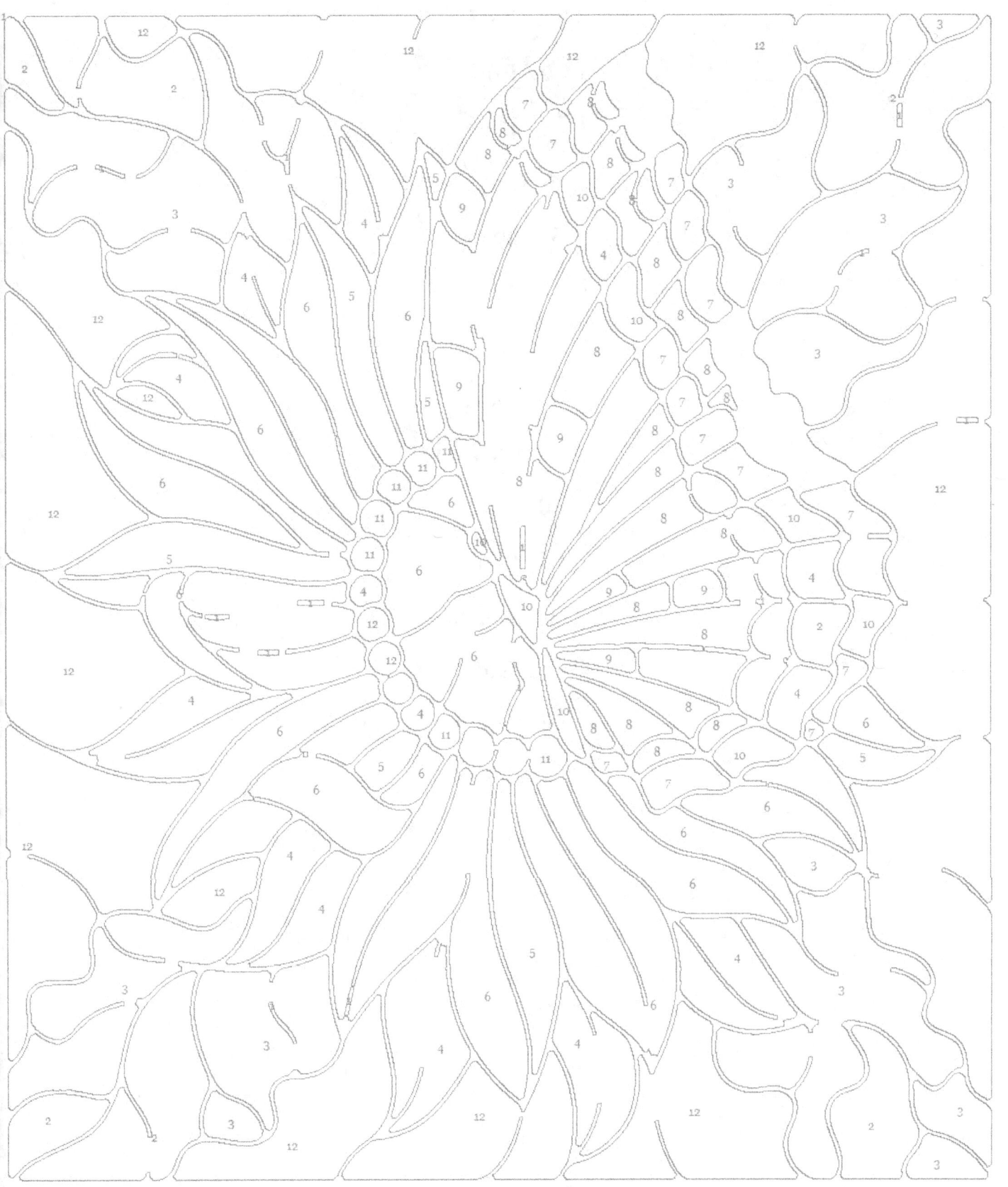

1. Red
2. Pink
3. Blue
4. Green
5. Purple
6. Light Blue
7. Light Green
8. Orange
9. Dark Red
10. Brown
11. Black
12. Dark Green
13. Gold
14. Violet
15. Yellow

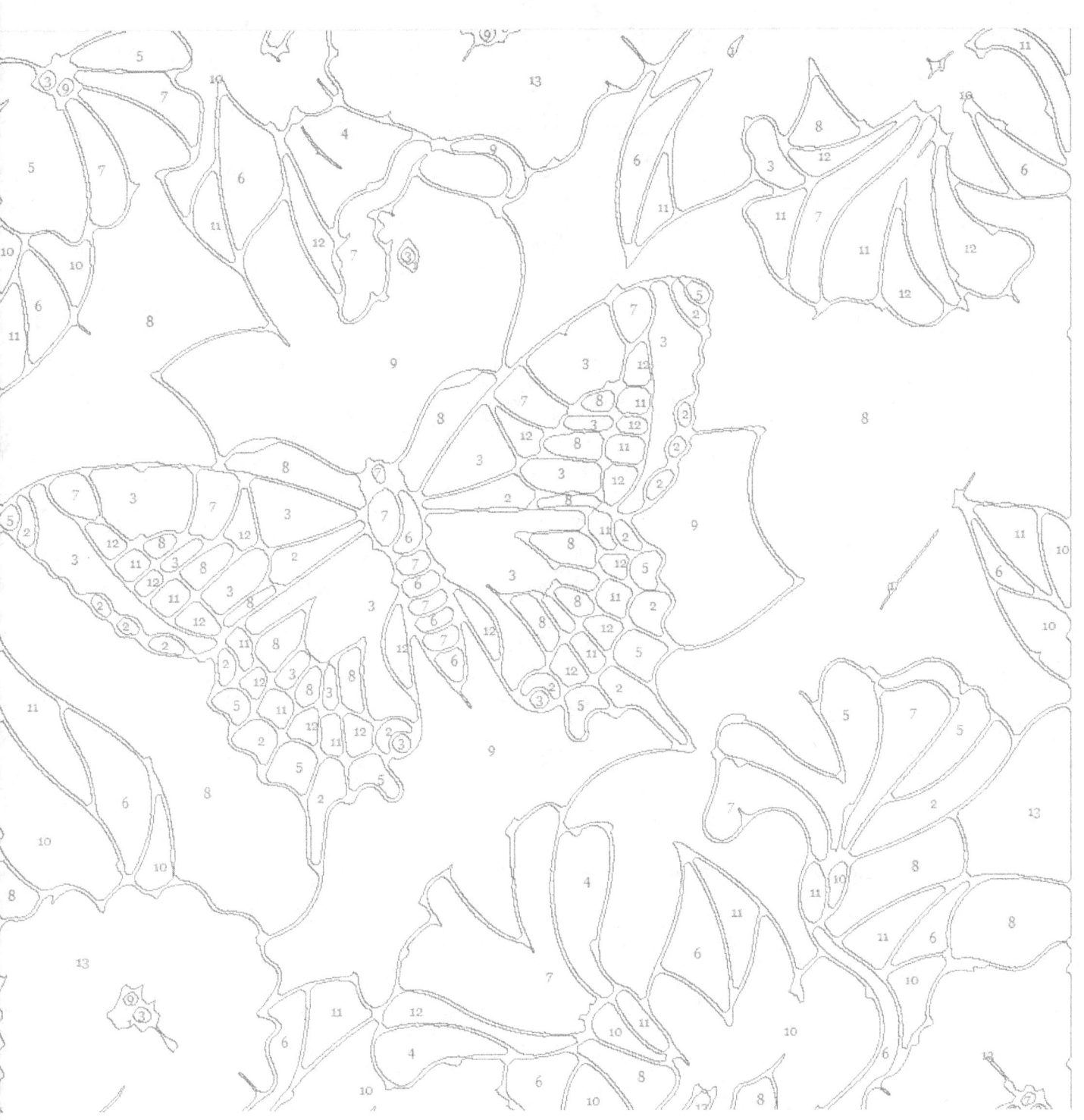

1. Red
2. Pink
3. Blue
4. Green
5. Purple
6. Light Blue
7. Light Green
8. Orange
9. Dark Red
10. Brown
11. Black
12. Dark Green
13. Gold
14. Violet
15. Yellow

1. Red
2. Pink
3. Blue
4. Green
5. Purple
6. Light Blue
7. Light Green
8. Orange
9. Dark Red
10. Brown
11. Black
12. Dark Green
13. Gold
14. Violet
15. Yellow

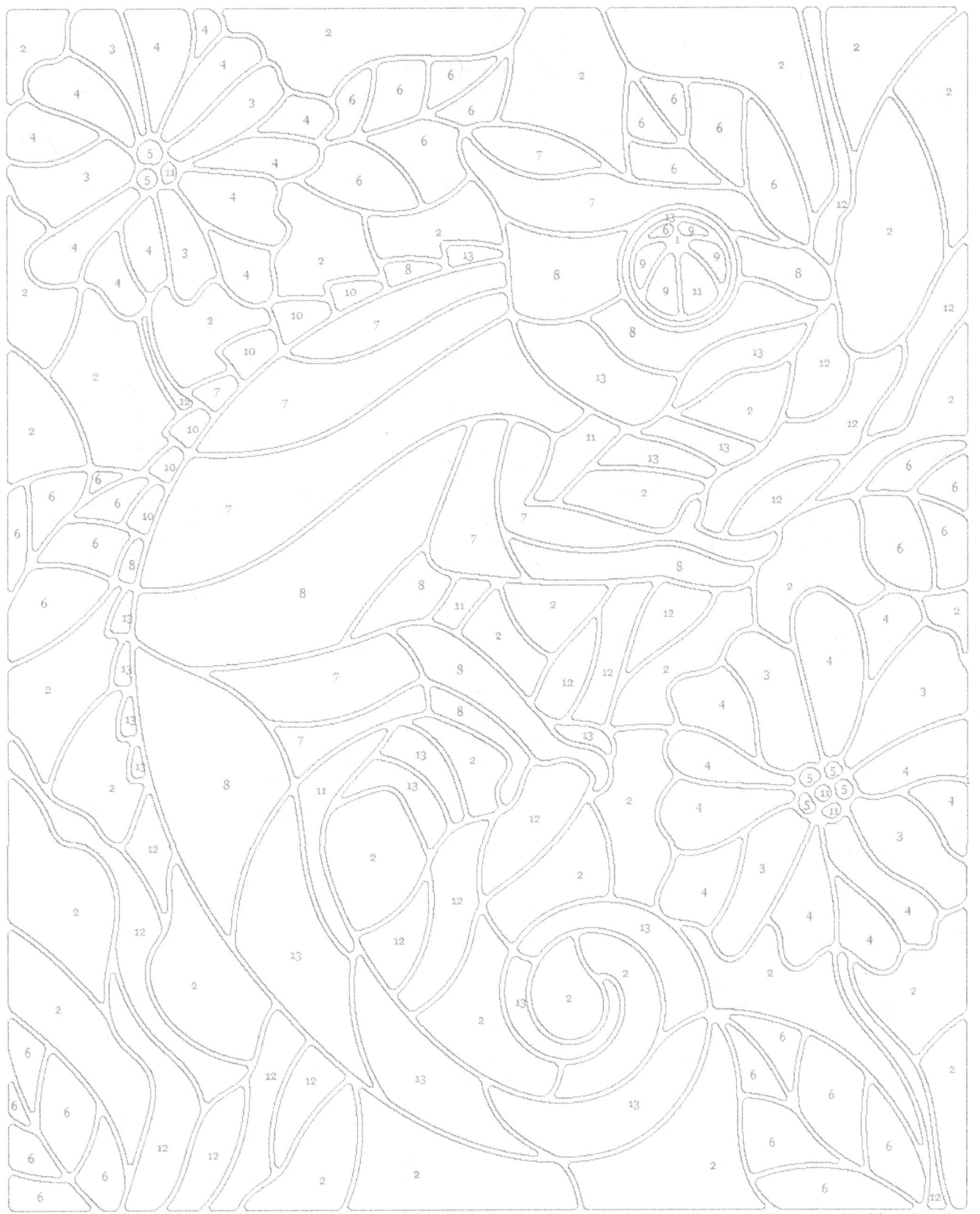

1. Red
2. Green
3. Brown
4. Pink
5. Purple
6. Grey
7. Light Green
8. Dark Red
9. Orange
10. Blue
11. Black
12. Dark Green
13. Gold
14. Violet
15. Yellow

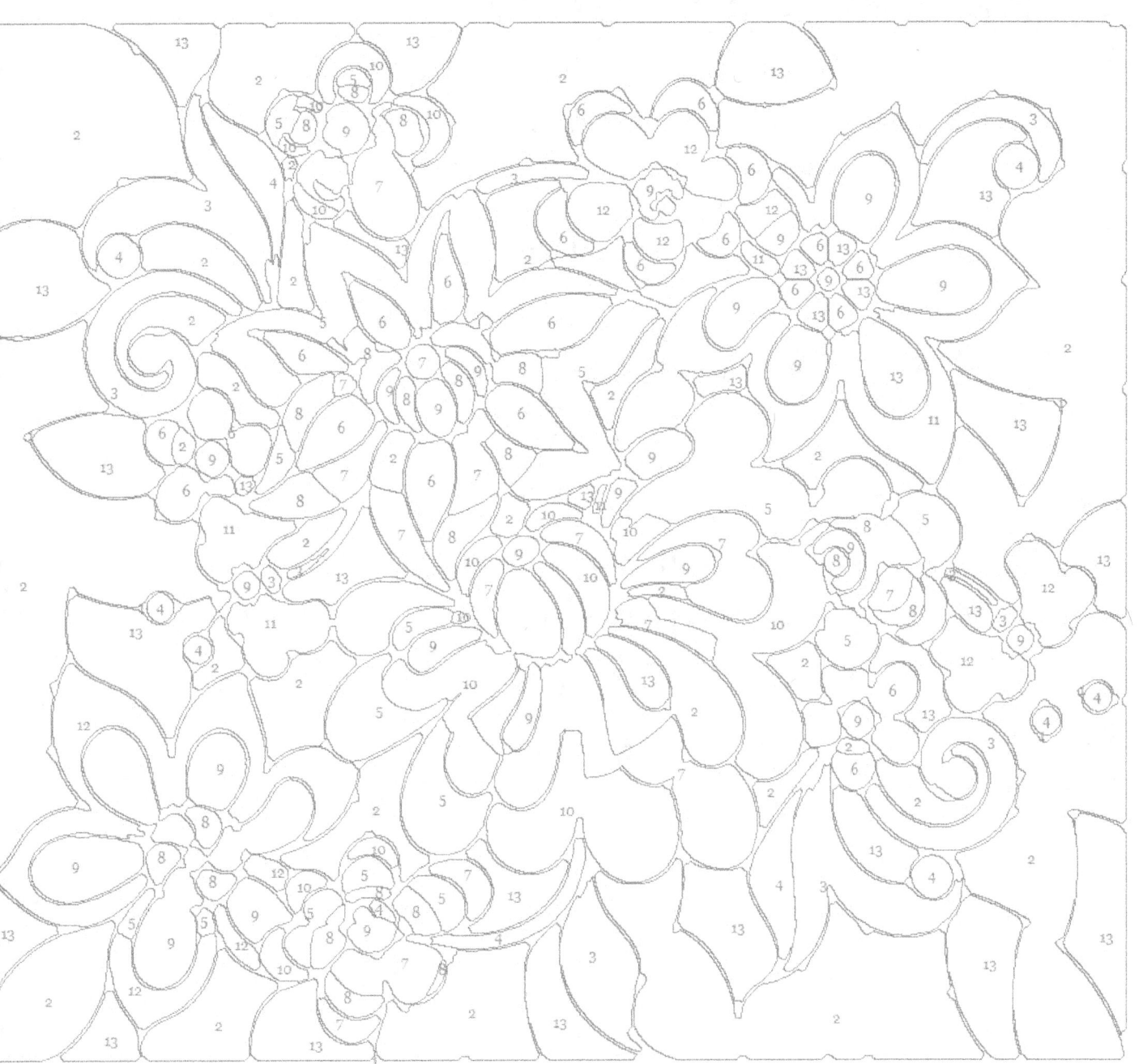

1. Red
2. Green
3. Brown
4. Pink
5. Purple
6. Grey
7. Light Green
8. Dark Red
9. Orange
10. Blue
11. Black
12. Dark Green
13. Gold
14. Violet
15. Yellow

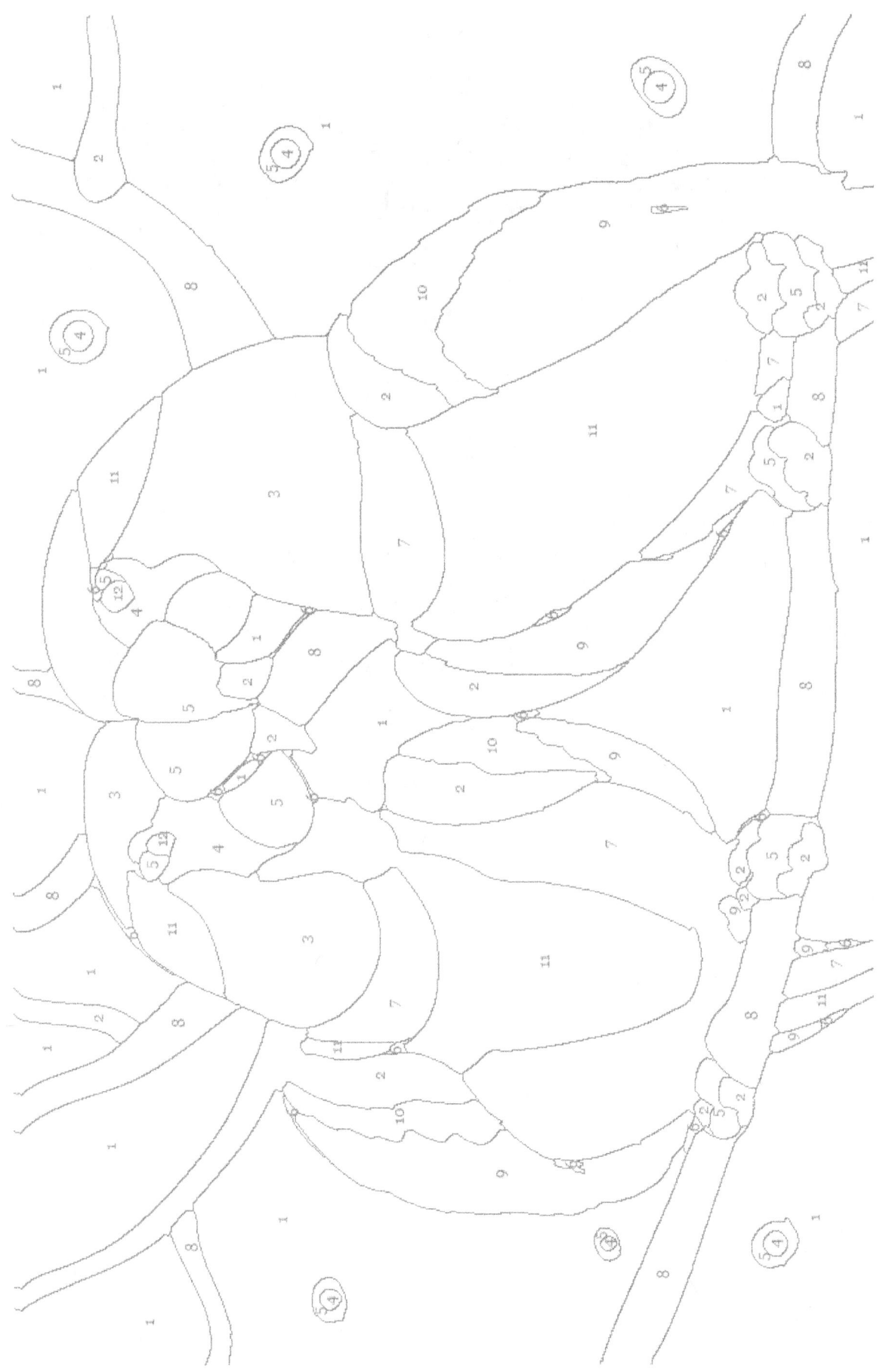

1. Blue
2. Green
3. Black
4. Pink
5. Orange
6. Light Blue
7. Light Green
8. Purple
9. Dark Red
10. Brown
11. Red
12. Dark Green
13. Gold
14. Violet
15. Yellow

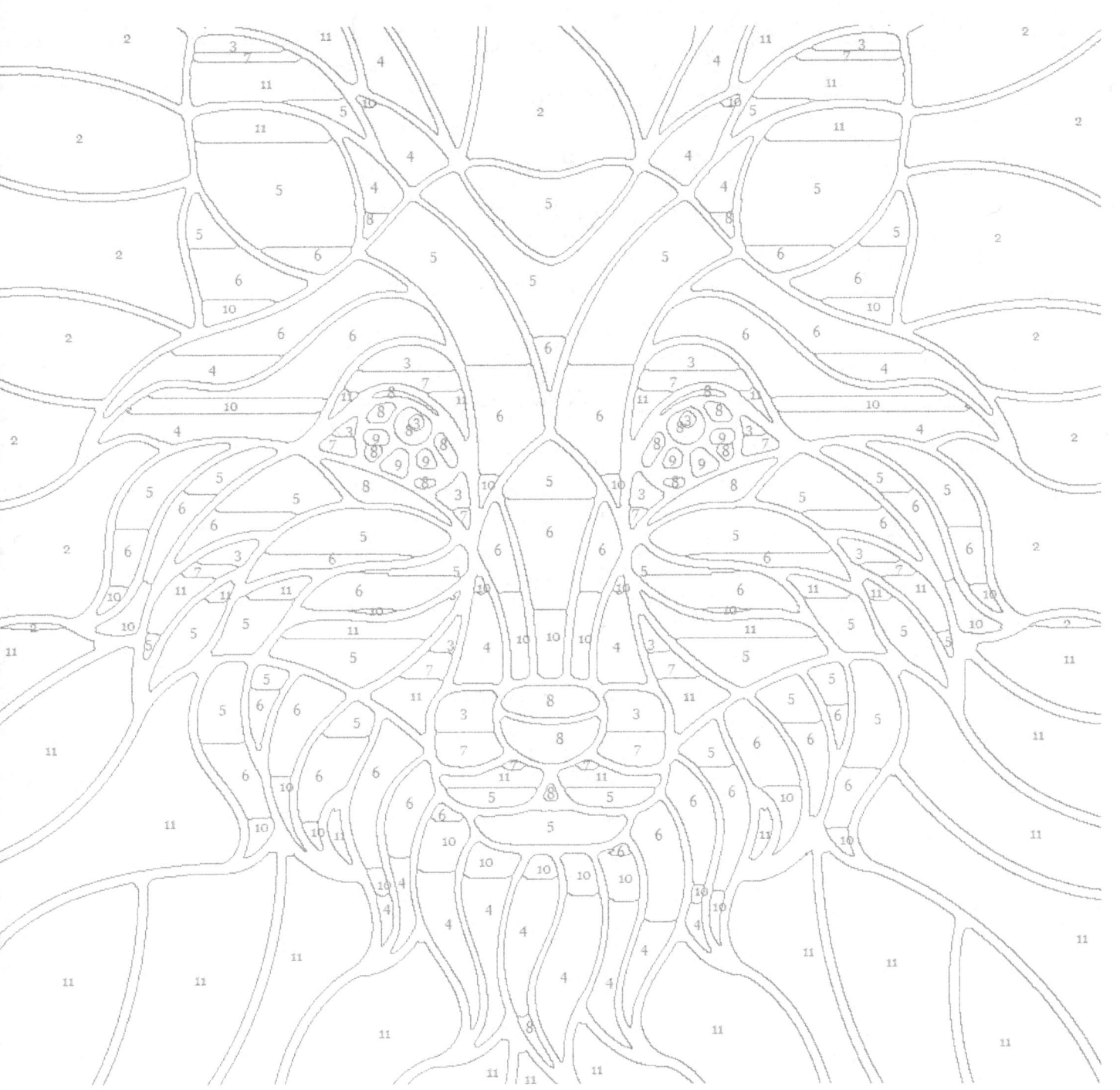

1. Red
2. Green
3. Blue
4. Pink
5. Purple
6. Light Blue
7. Light Green
8. Orange
9. Dark Red
10. Brown
11. Black
12. Dark Green
13. Gold
14. Violet
15. Yellow

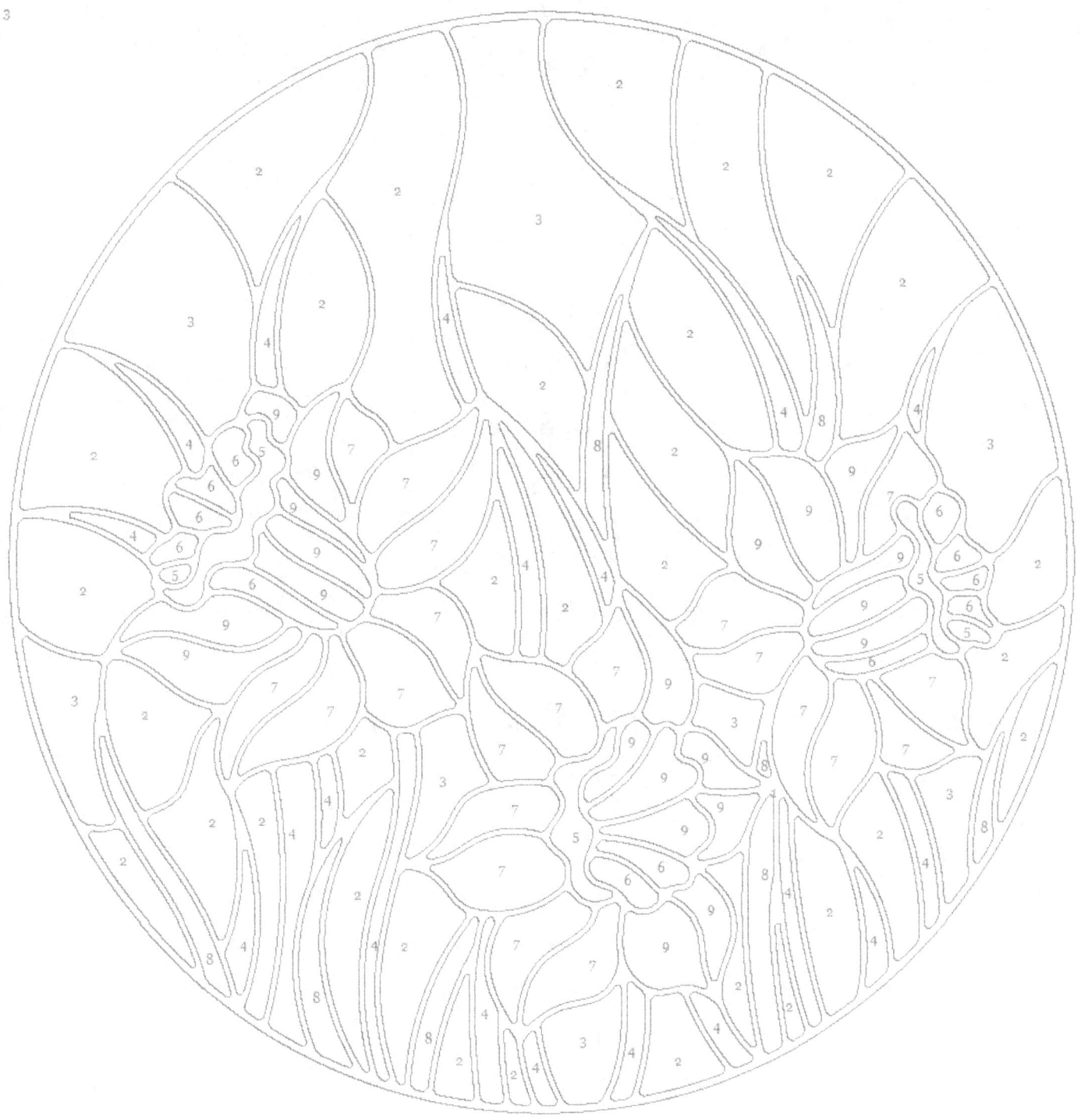

1. Red
2. Green
3. Blue
4. Pink
5. Purple
6. Light Blue
7. Light Green
8. Orange
9. Dark Red
10. Brown
11. Black
12. Dark Green
13. Gold
14. Violet
15. Yellow

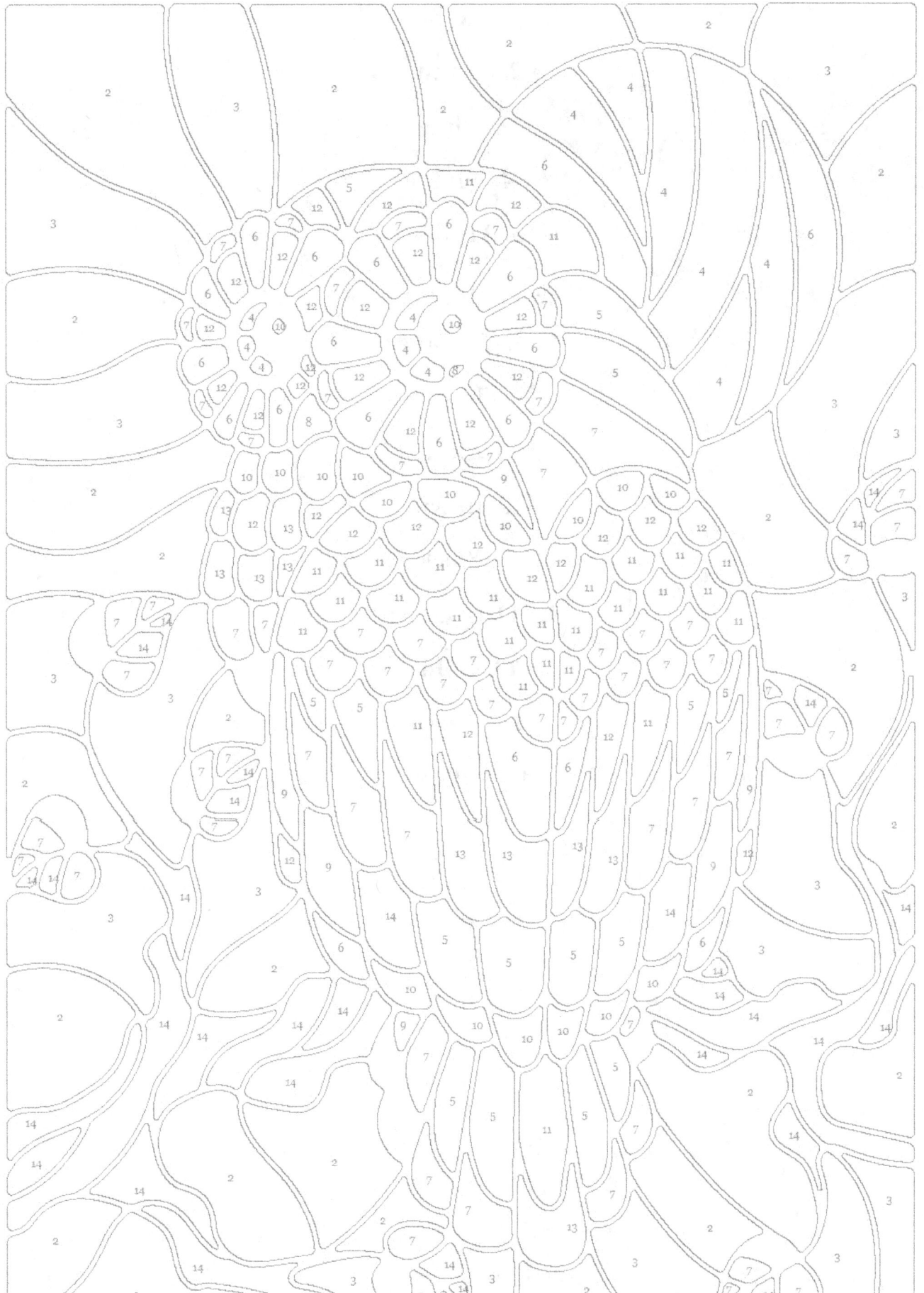

1. Red
2. Green
3. Blue
4. Pink
5. Purple
6. Light Blue
7. Light Green
8. Orange
9. Dark Red
10. Brown
11. Black
12. Dark Green
13. Gold
14. Violet
15. Yellow

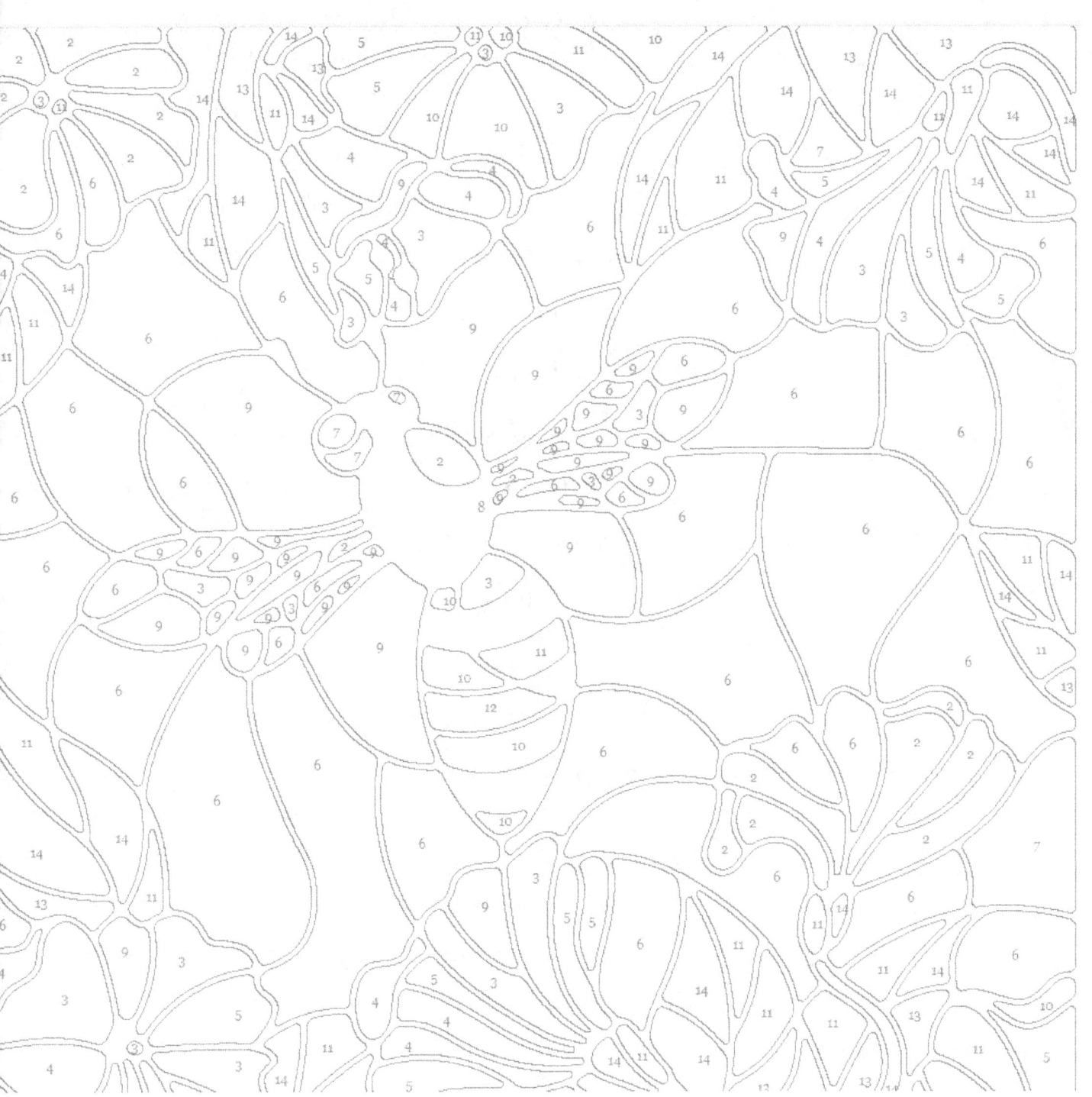

1. Red
2. Green
3. Blue
4. Pink
5. Purple
6. Light Blue
7. Light Green
8. Black
9. Dark Red
10. Orange
11. Brown
12. Yellow
13. Gold
14. Violet
15. Dark Green

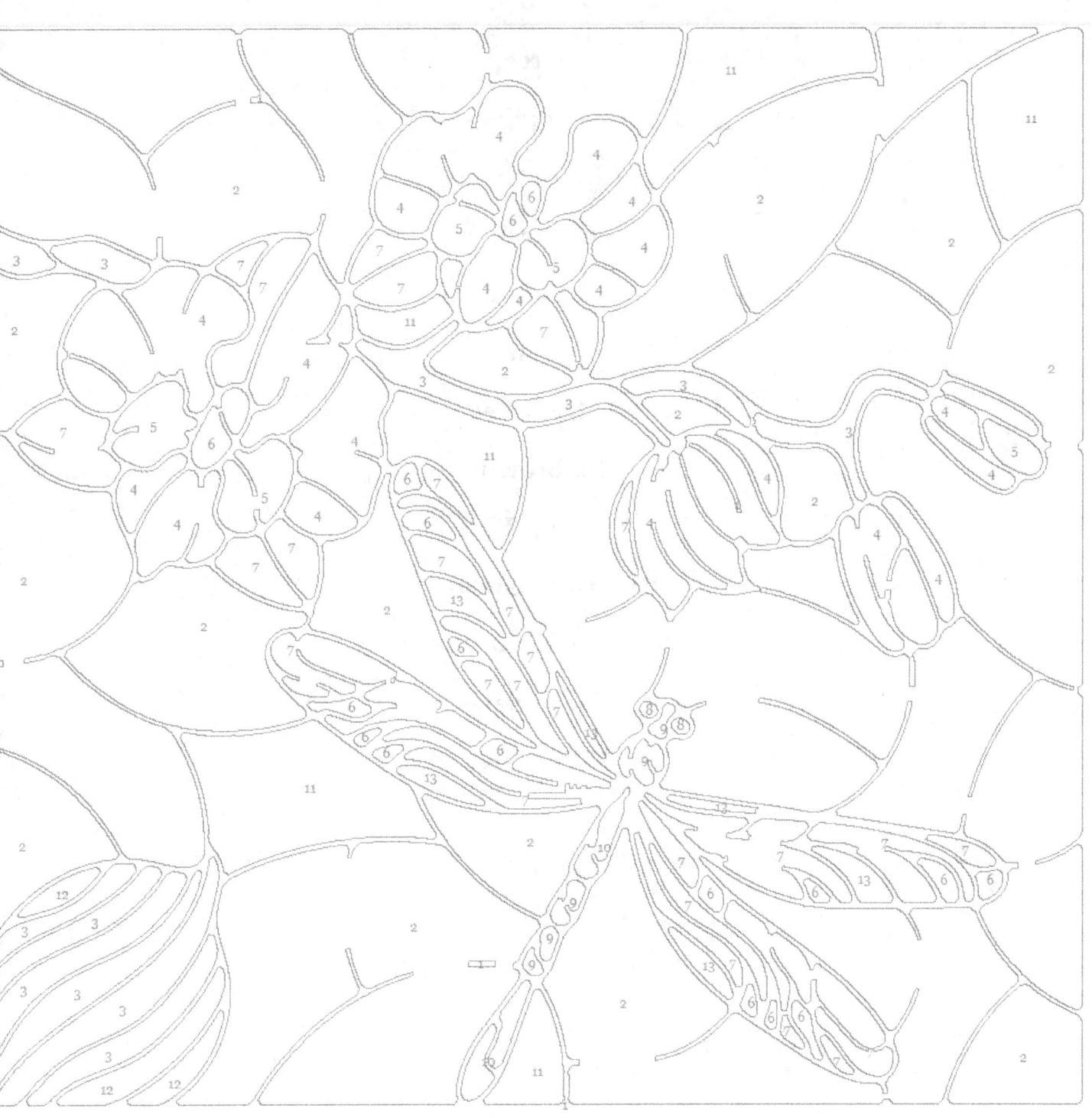

1. Red
2. Blue
3. Green
4. Pink
5. Light Green
6. Black
7. Purple
8. Orange
9. Dark Red
10. Brown
11. Light Blue
12. Dark Green
13. Gold
14. Violet
15. Yellow

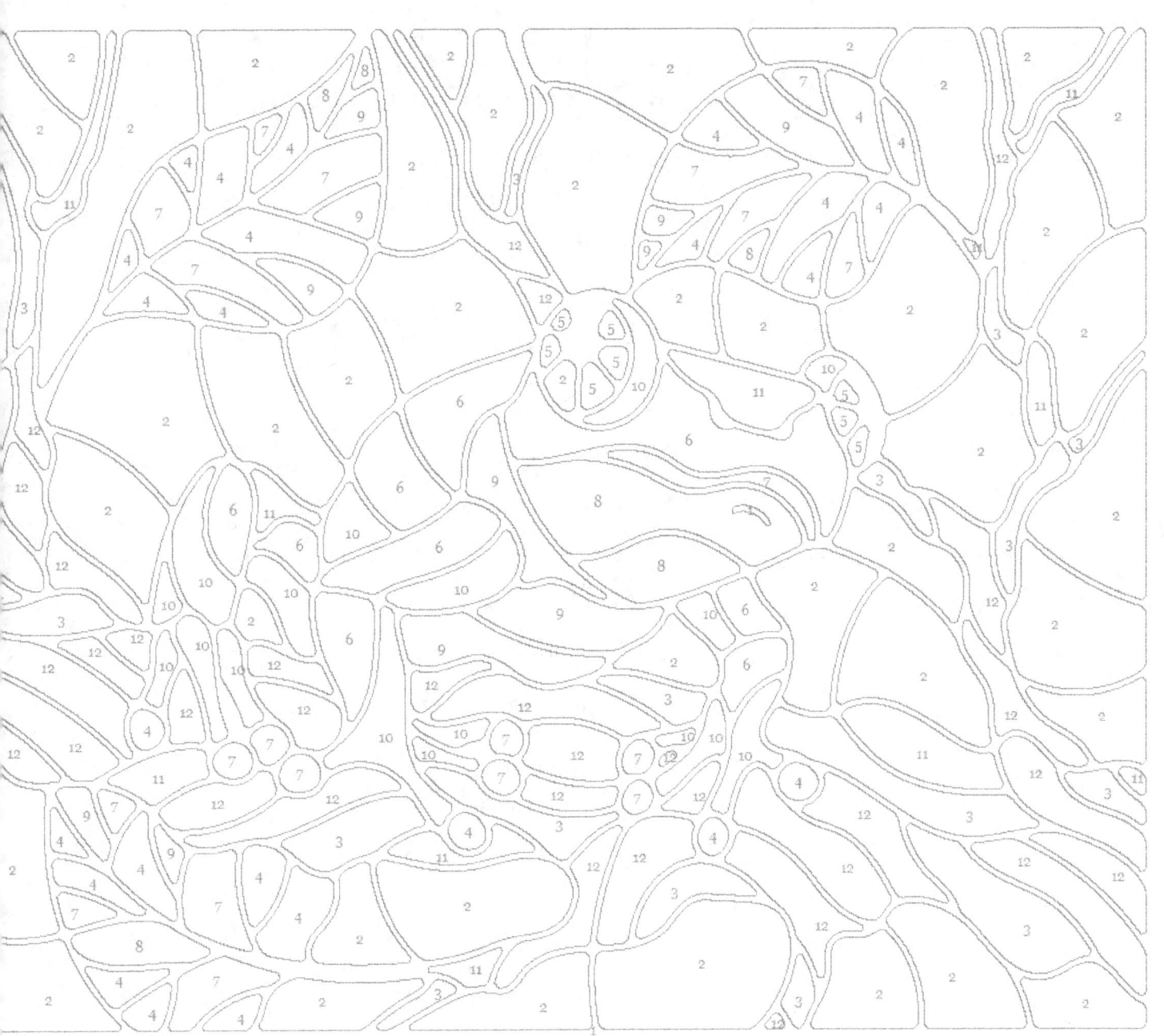

1. Light Blue
2. Blue
3. Green
4. Dark Green
5. Purple
6. Red
7. Light Green
8. Orange
9. Dark Red
10. Pink
11. Black
12. Brown
13. Gold
14. Violet
15. Yellow

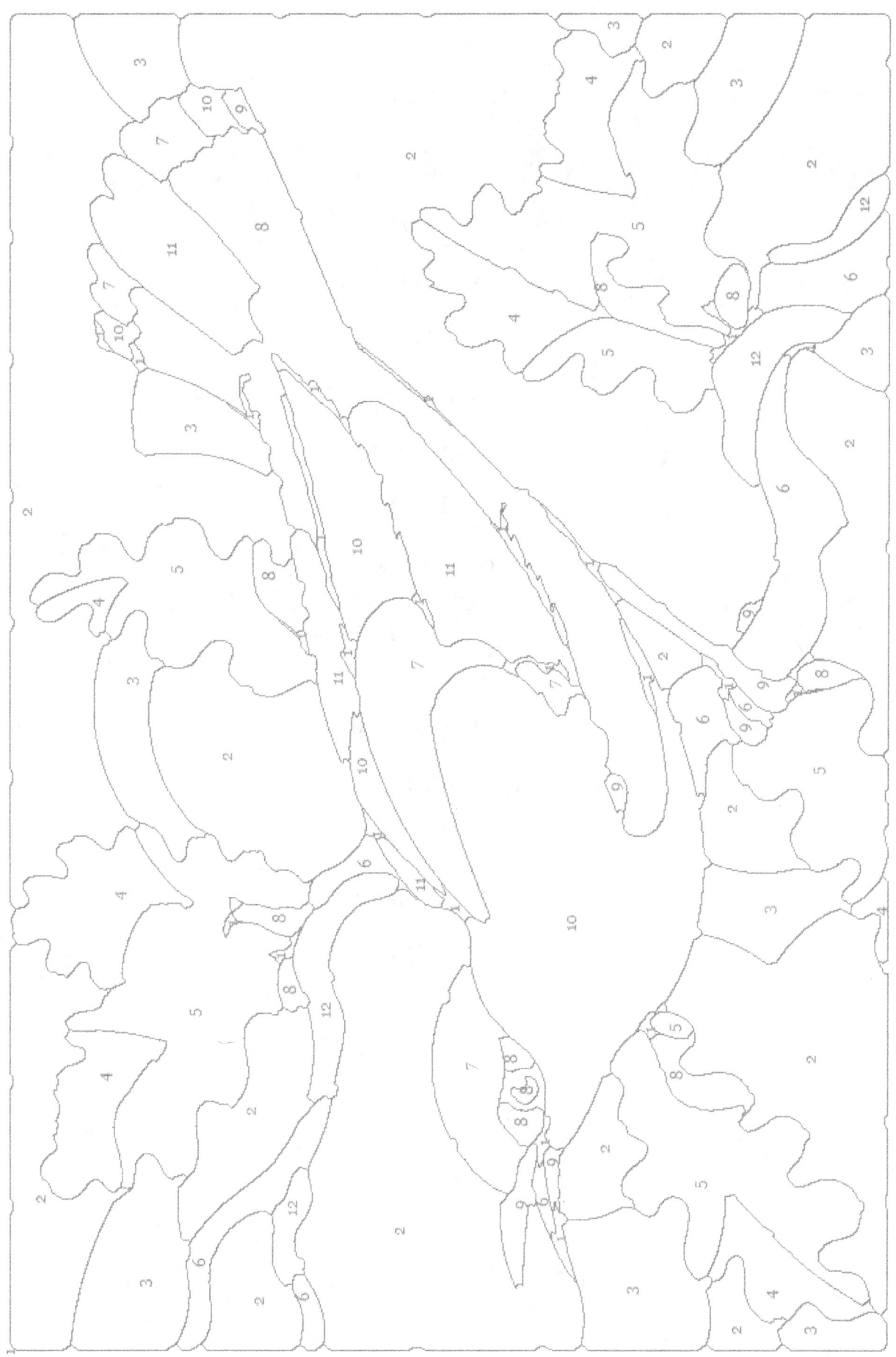

1. Red
2. Blue
3. Green
4. Pink
5. Purple
6. Light Blue
7. Black
8. Orange
9. Dark Red
10. Brown
11. Light green
12. Dark Green
13. Gold
14. Violet
15. Yellow

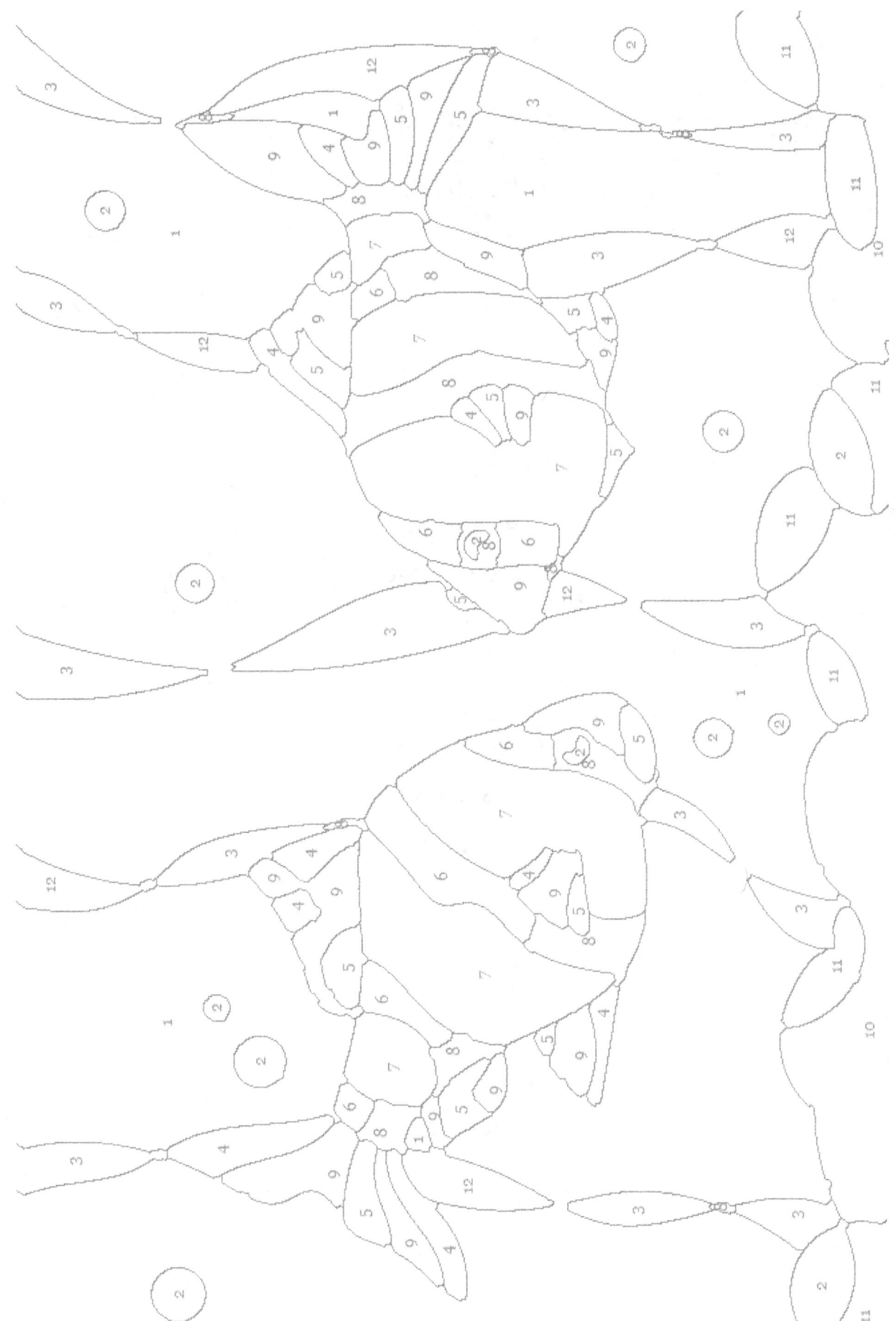

1. Red
2. Green
3. Blue
4. Pink
5. Purple
6. Light Blue
7. Light Green
8. Orange
9. Dark Red
10. Brown
11. Black
12. Dark Green
13. Gold
14. Violet
15. Yellow

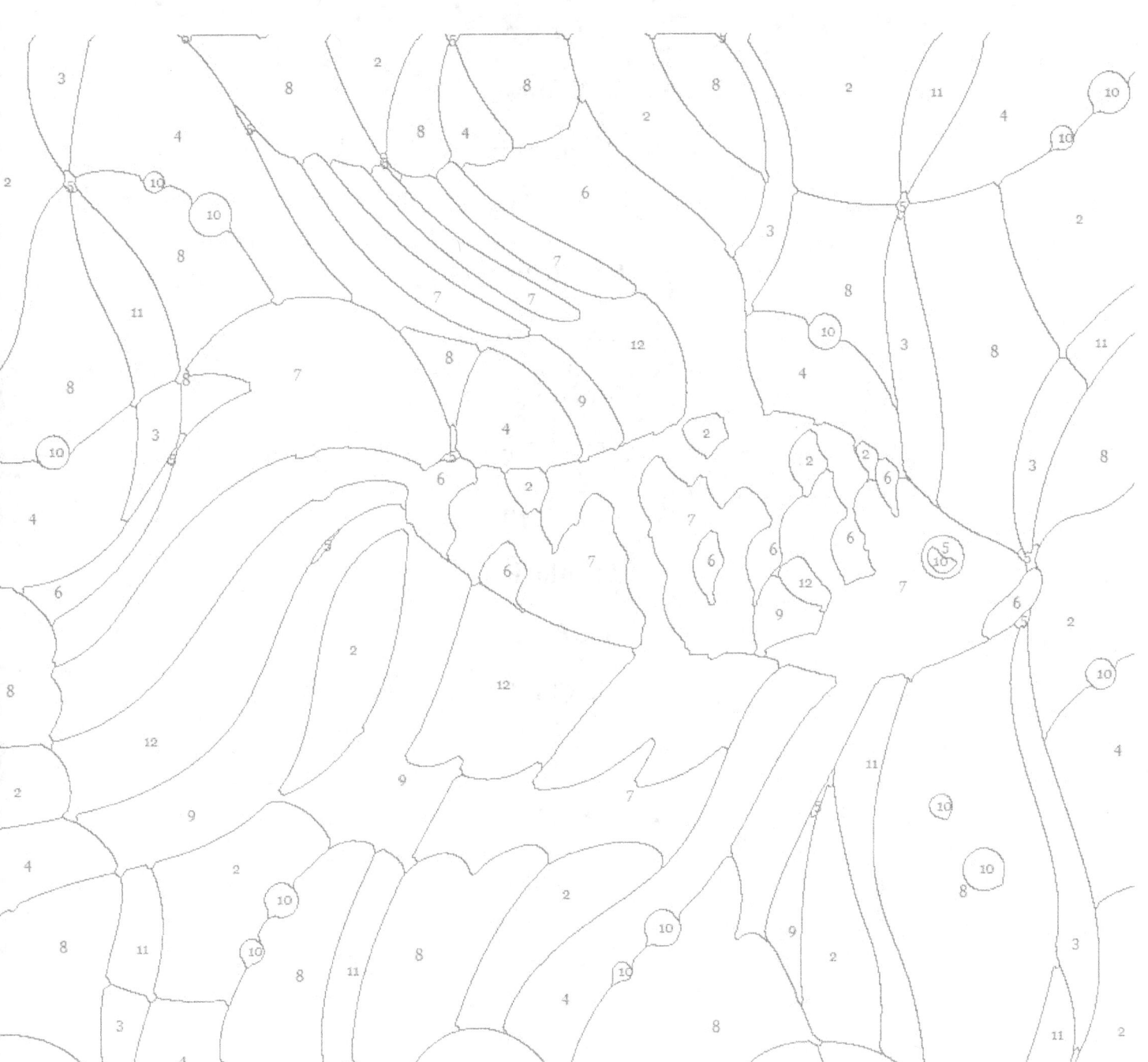

1. Red
2. Green
3. Yellow
4. Light Blue
5. Dark Blue
6. Purple
7. Light Green
8. Orange
9. Dark Red
10. Brown
11. Black
12. Blue
13. Gold
14. Violet
15. Dark Green

1. Red
2. Green
3. Yellow
4. Light Blue
5. Dark Blue
6. Purple
7. Light Green
8. Orange
9. Dark Red
10. Brown
11. Black
12. Blue
13. Gold
14. Violet
15. Dark Green

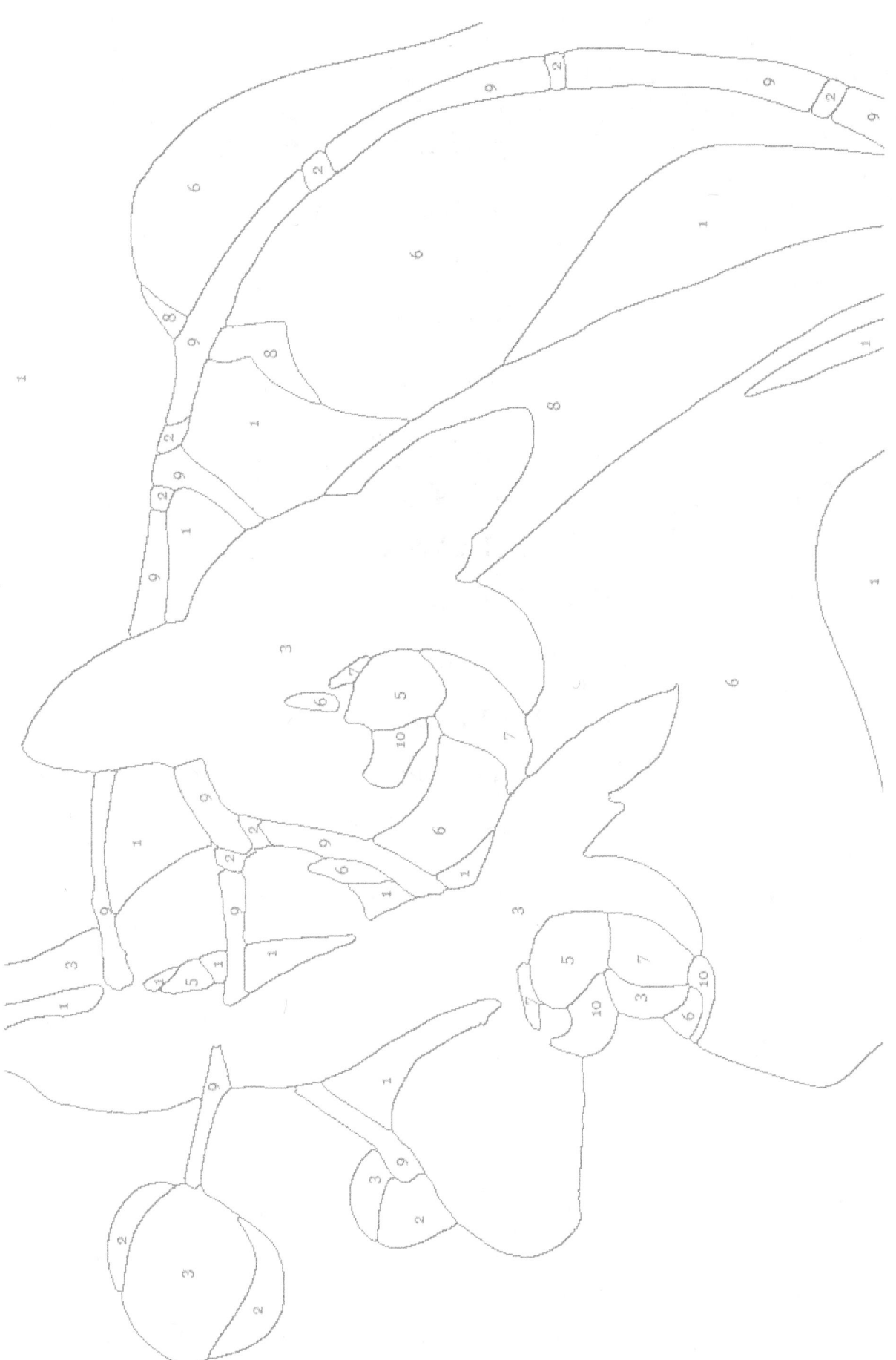

1. Red
2. Green
3. Blue
4. Pink
5. Purple
6. Light Blue
7. Light Green
8. Orange
9. Dark Red
10. Brown
11. Black
12. Dark Green
13. Gold
14. Violet
15. Yellow

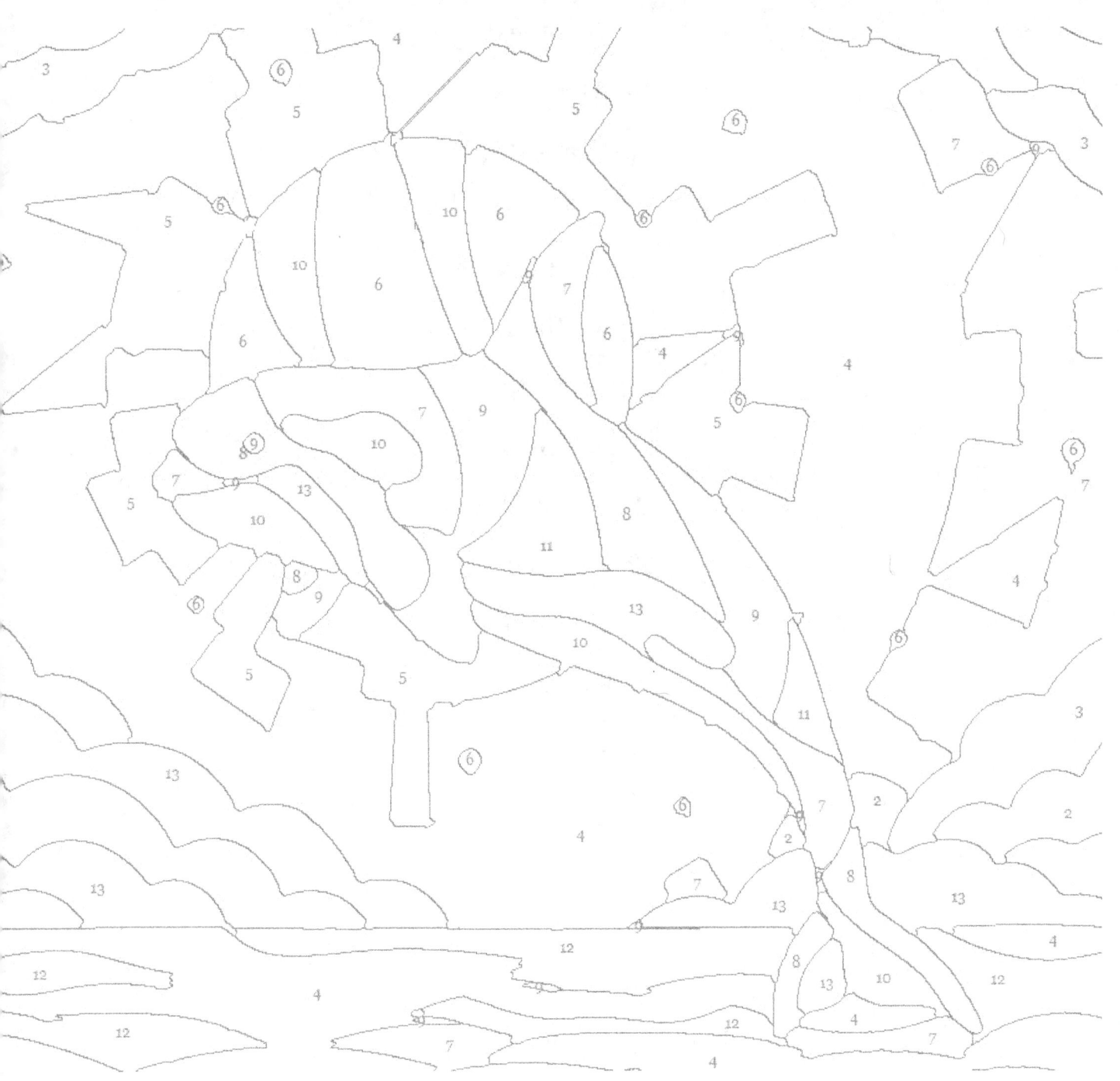

1. Red
2. Green
3. Blue
4. Dark Blue
5. Dark Red
6. Orange
7. Light Green
8. Black
9. Purple
10. Yellow
11. Light Blue
12. Dark Green
13. Gold
14. Violet
15. Brown

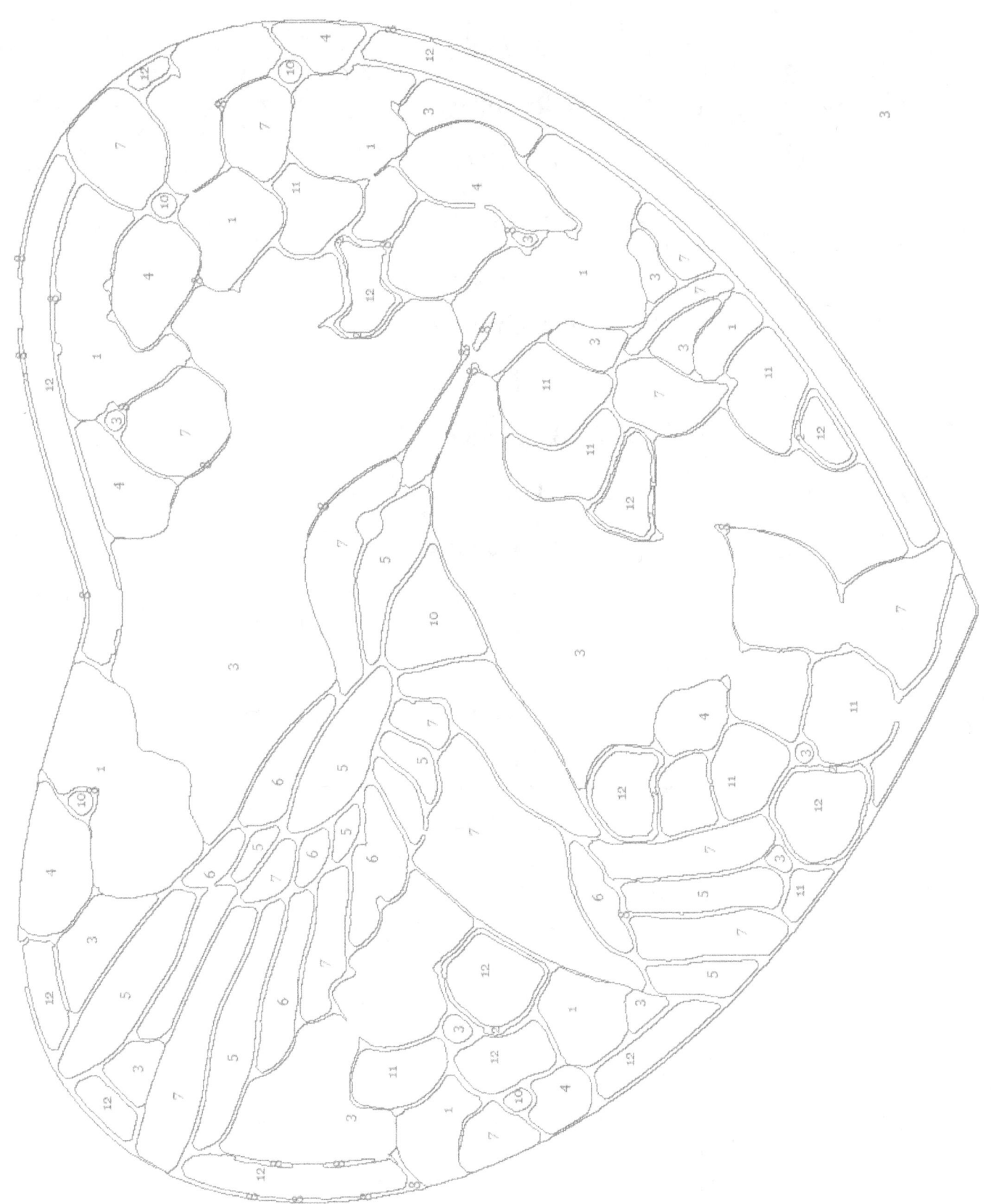

1. Red
2. Green
3. Blue
4. Pink
5. Purple
6. Light Blue
7. Light Green
8. Orange
9. Dark Red
10. Brown
11. Black
12. Dark Green
13. Gold
14. Violet
15. Yellow

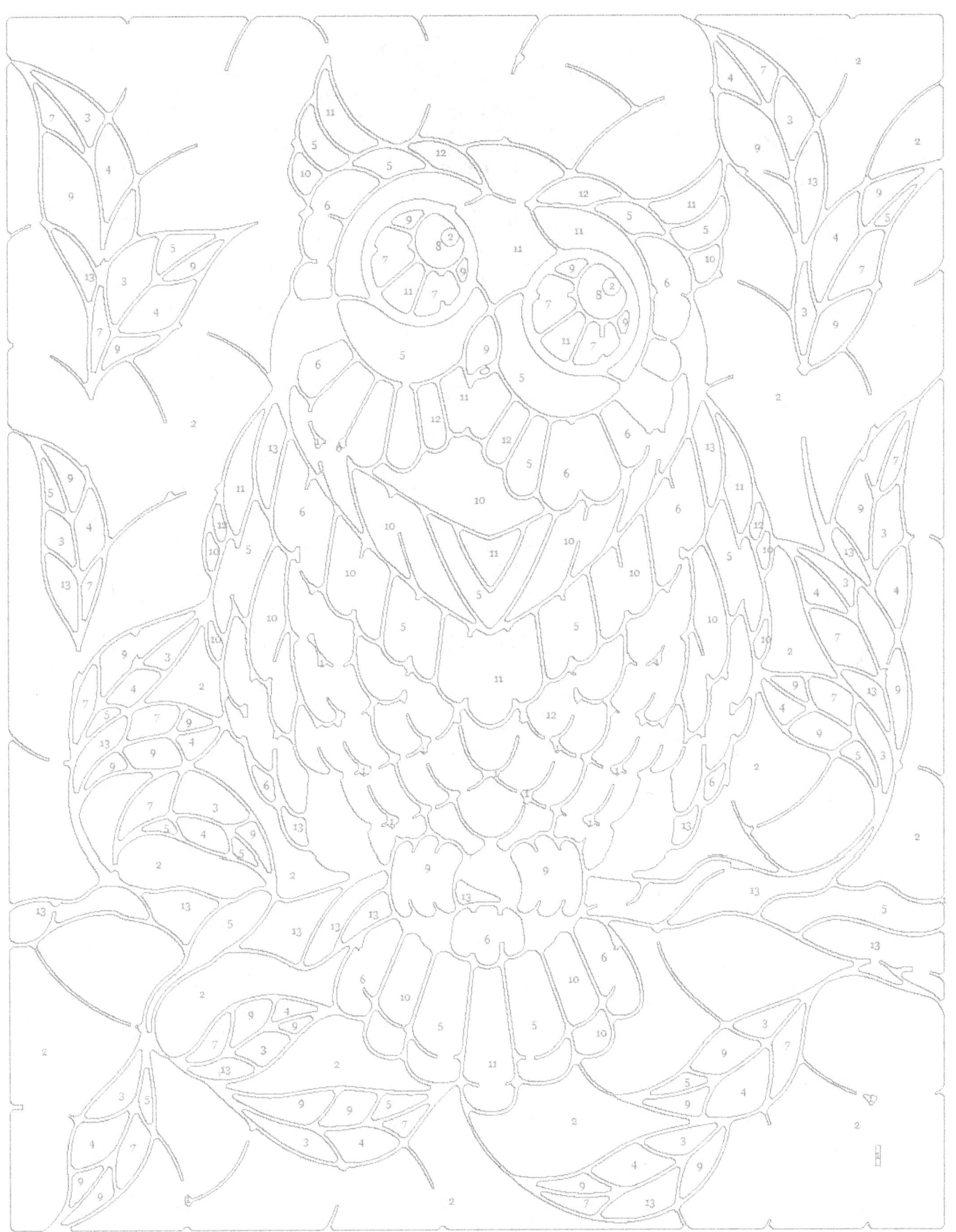

1. Red
2. Green
3. Blue
4. Pink
5. Purple
6. Light Blue
7. Light Green
8. Orange
9. Dark Red
10. Brown
11. Black
12. Dark Green
13. Gold
14. Violet
15. Yellow

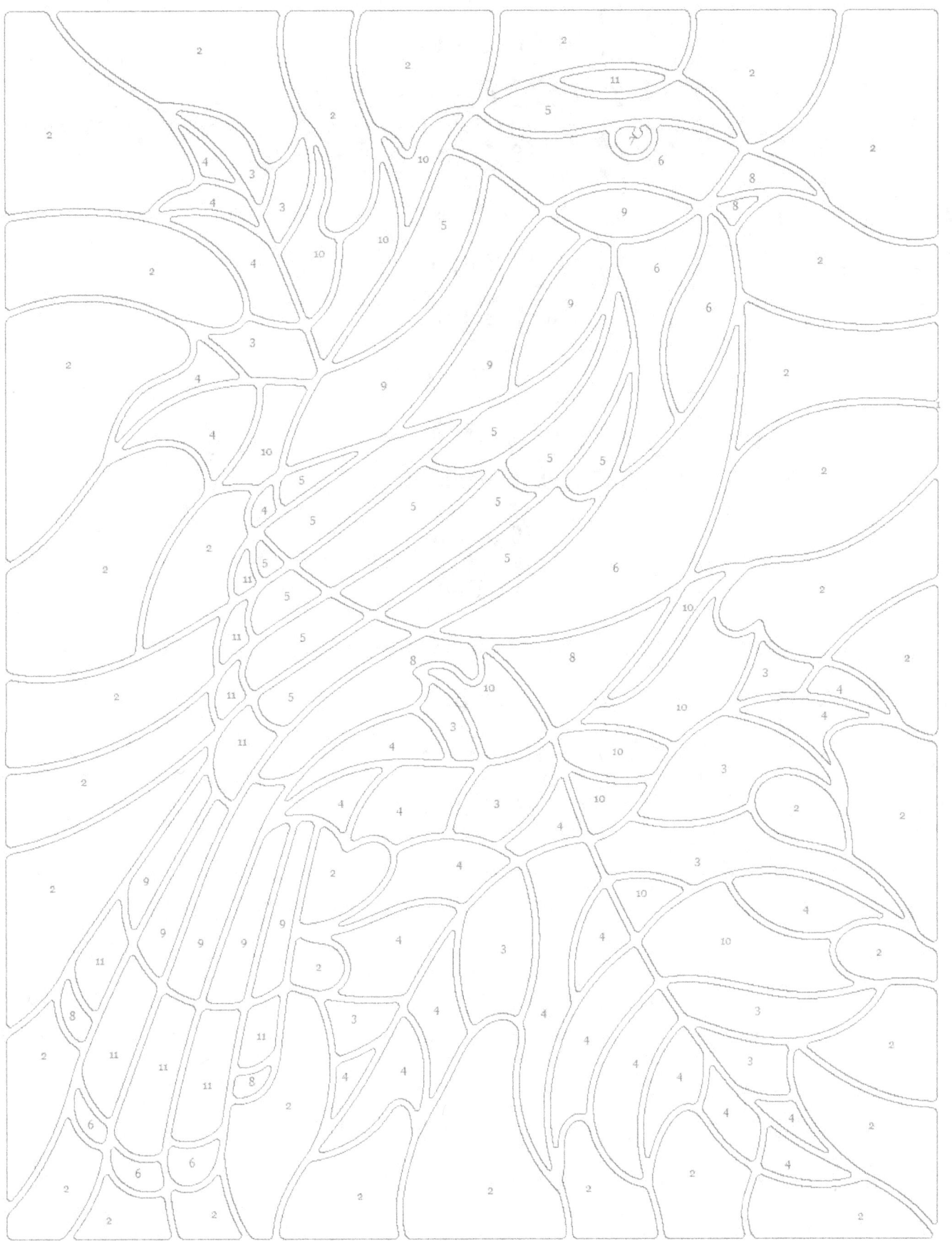

1. Black
2. Green
3. Blue
4. Pink
5. Purple
6. Light Blue
7. Light Green
8. Orange
9. Dark Red
10. Brown
11. Red
12. Dark Green
13. Gold
14. Violet
15. Yellow

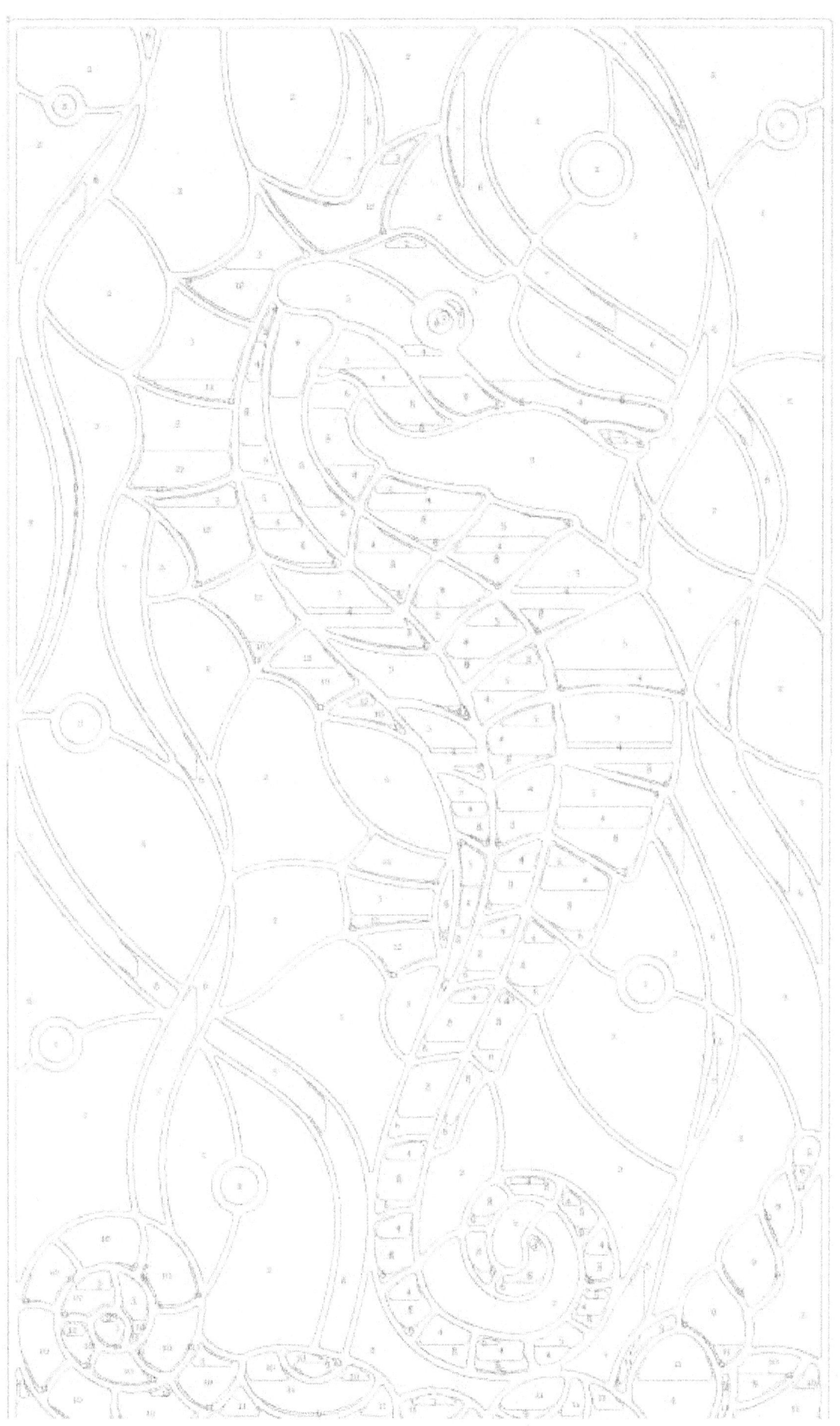

1. Black
2. Green
3. Blue
4. Pink
5. Purple
6. Light Blue
7. Light Green
8. Orange
9. Dark Red
10. Brown
11. Red
12. Dark Green
13. Gold
14. Violet
15. Yellow

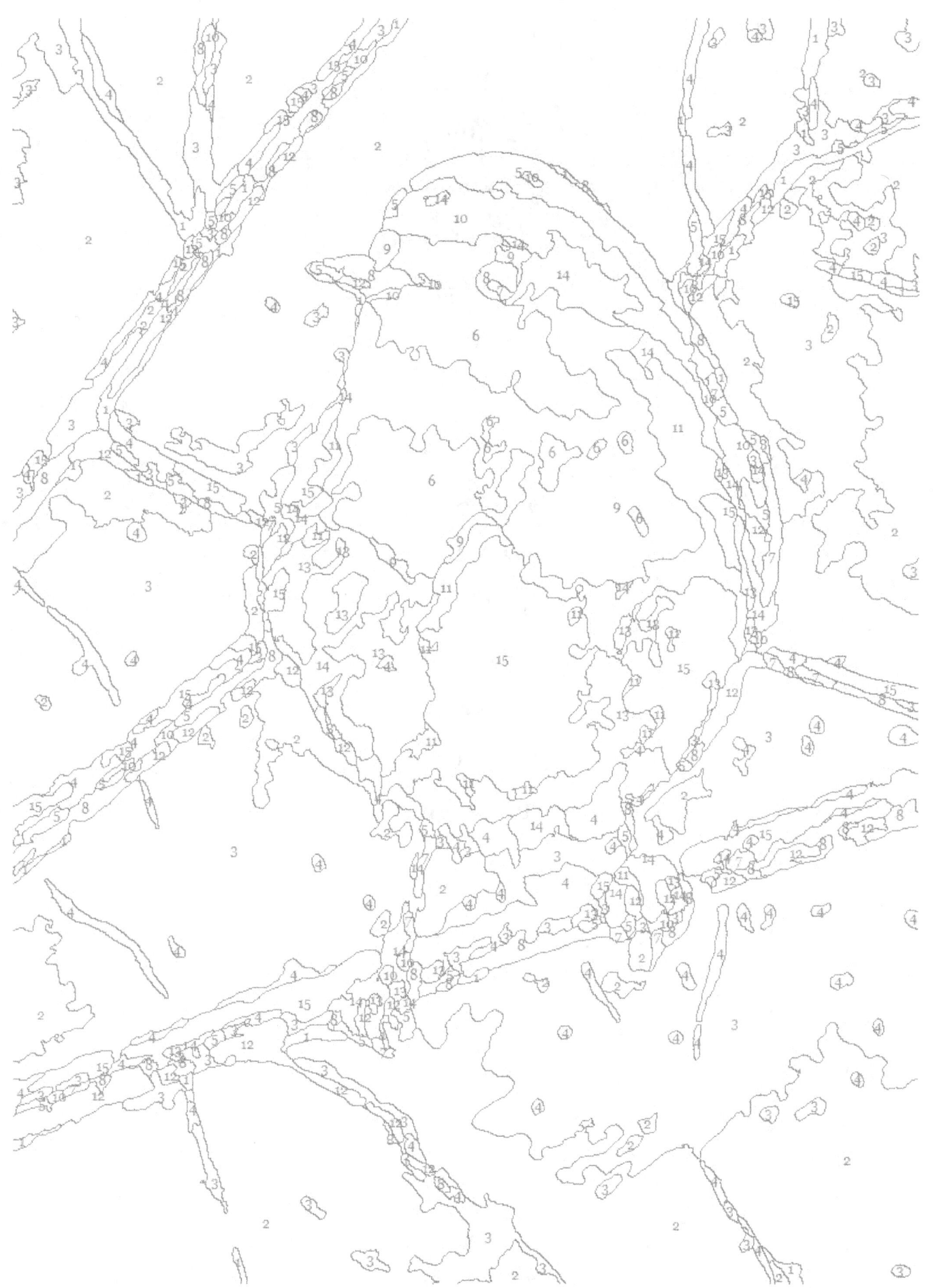

1. Black
2. Blue
3. Green
4. Light Green
5. Purple
6. Red
7. Pink
8. Orange
9. Dark Red
10. Brown
11. Light Blue
12. Dark Green
13. Gold
14. Violet
15. Yellow

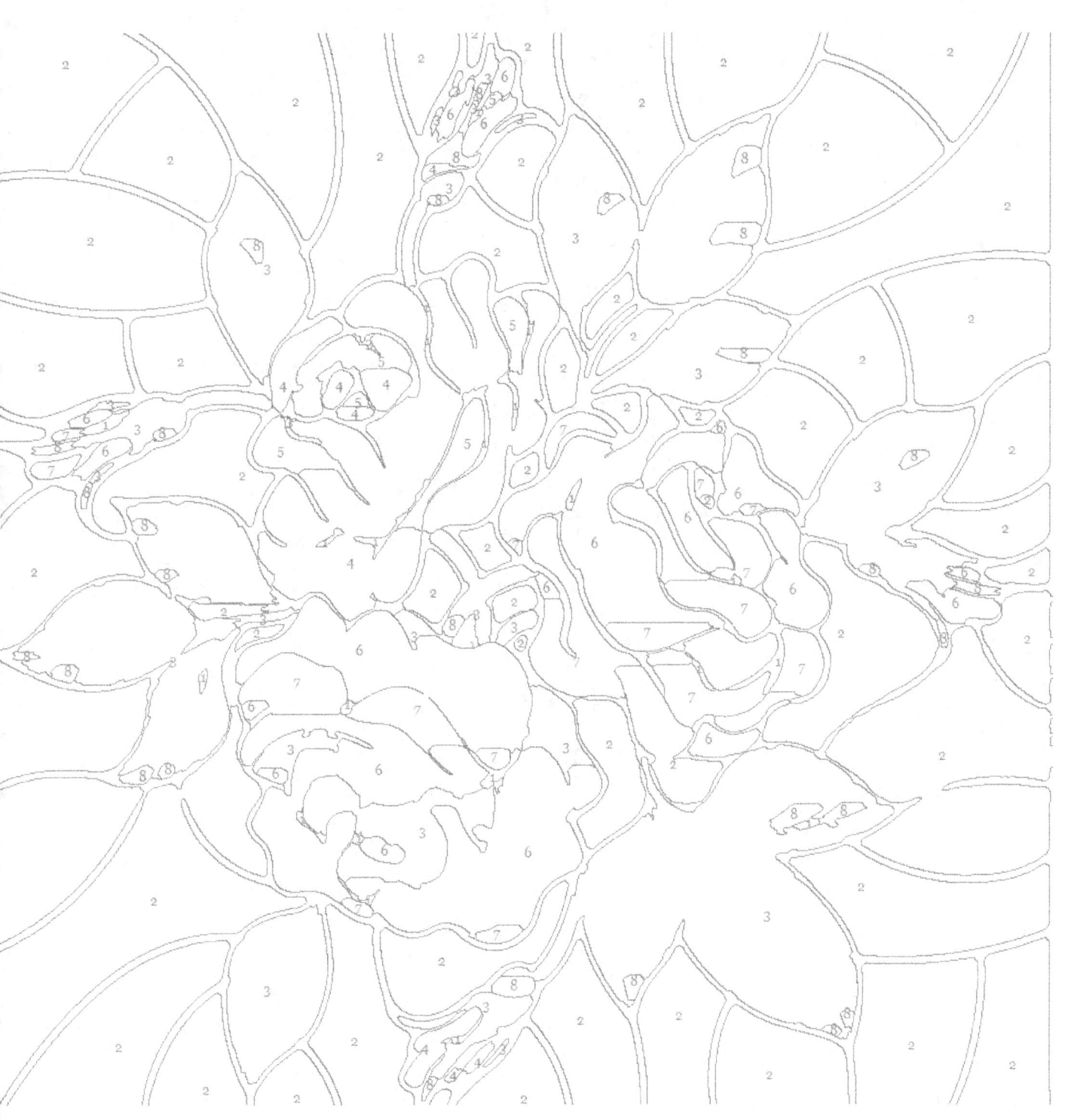

1. Black
2. Orange
3. Yellow
4. Violet
5. Purple
6. Light Blue
7. Light Green
8. Green
9. Dark Red
10. Purple
11. Blue
12. Dark Green
13. Gold
14. Brown
15. Red

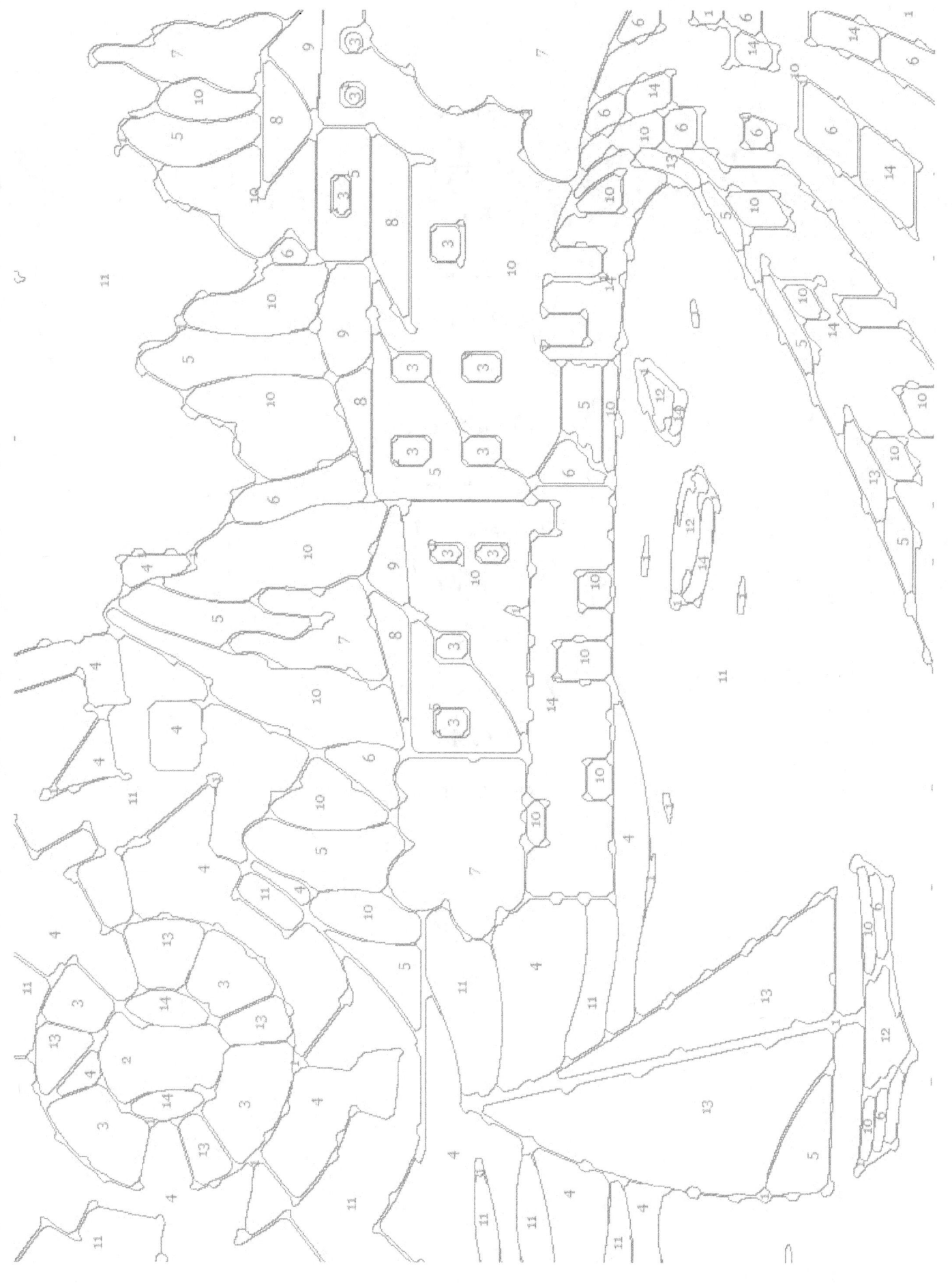

1. Black
2. Green
3. Blue
4. Pink
5. Purple
6. Light Blue
7. Light Green
8. Orange
9. Dark Red
10. Brown
11. Red
12. Dark Green
13. Gold
14. Violet
15. Yellow

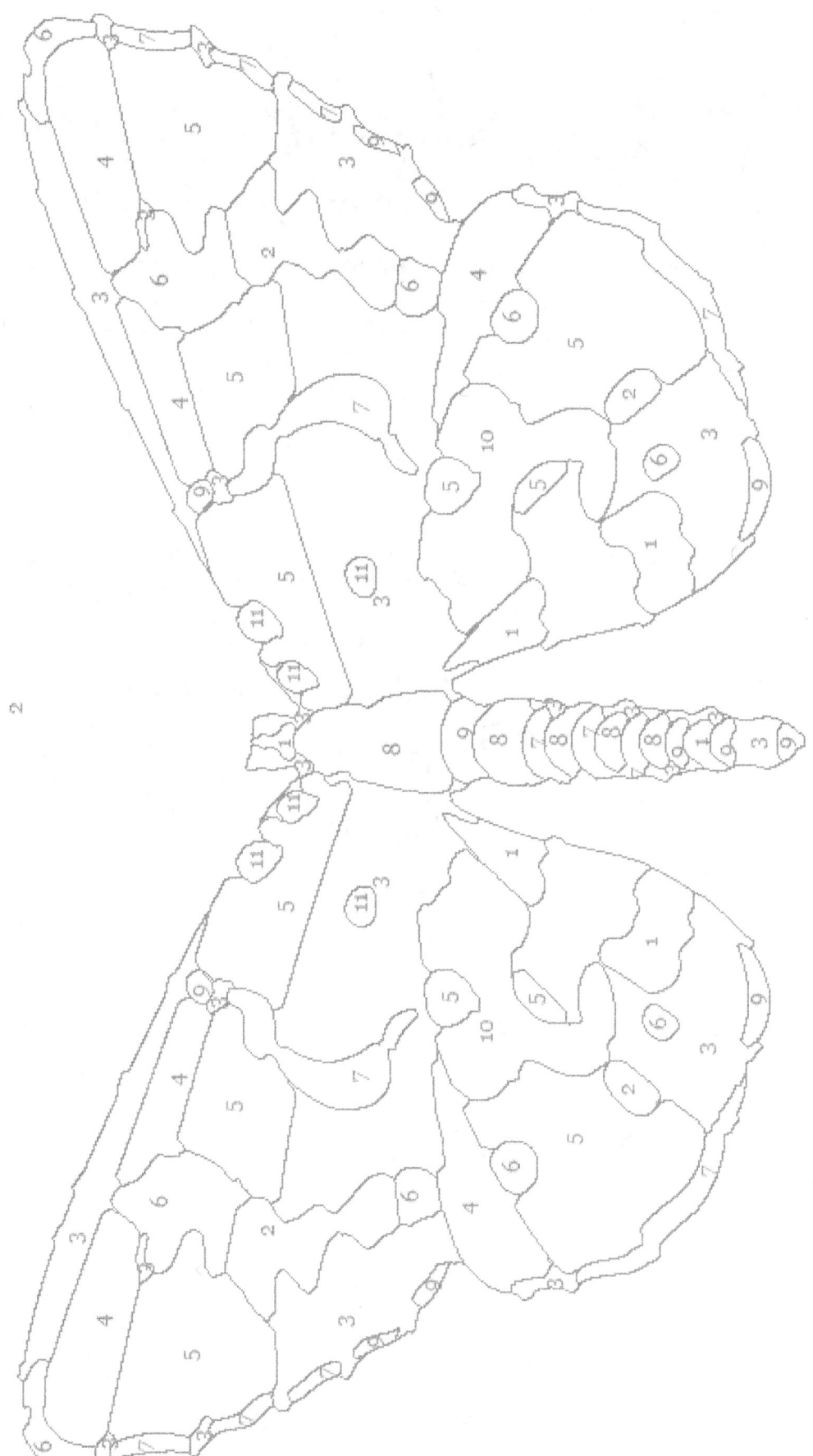

1. Black
2. Dark Green
3. Blue
4. Brown
5. Purple
6. Light Blue
7. Light Green
8. Orange
9. Dark Red
10. Green
11. Red
12. Pink
13. Gold
14. Violet
15. Yellow

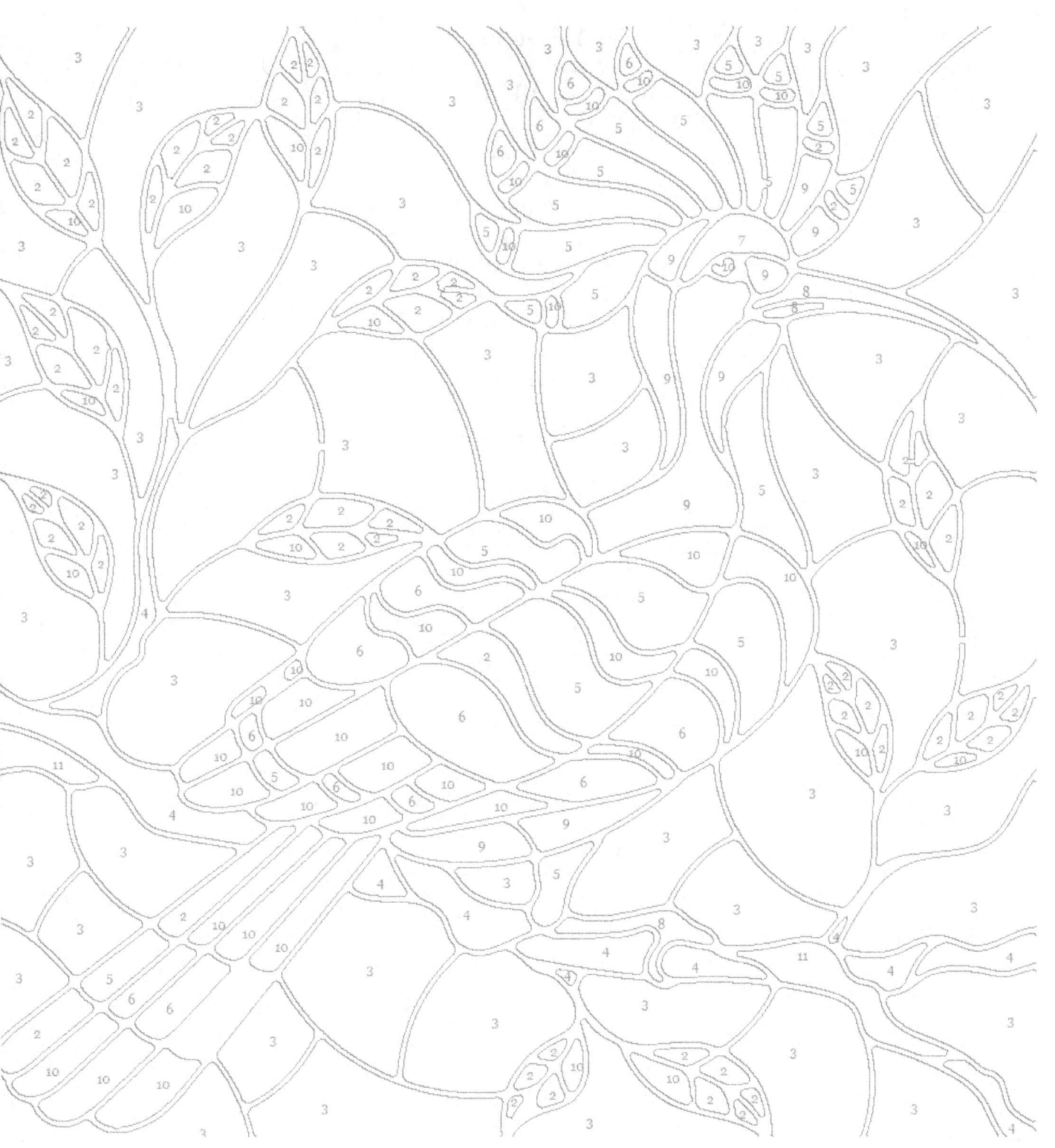

1. Black
2. Green
3. Blue
4. Pink
5. Purple
6. Light Blue
7. Light Green
8. Orange
9. Dark Red
10. Brown
11. Red
12. Dark Green
13. Gold
14. Violet
15. Yellow

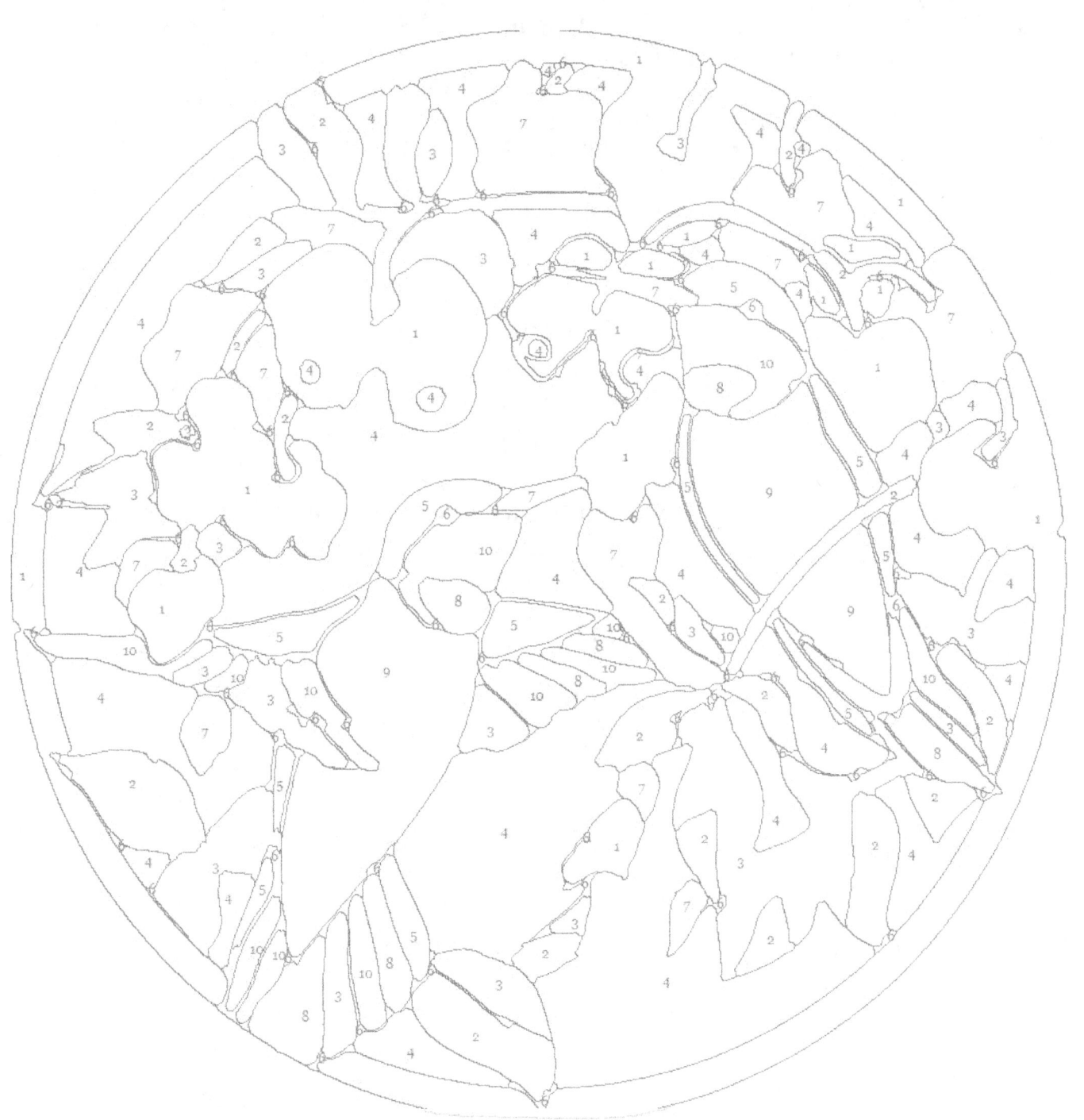

1. Black
2. Blue
3. Purple
4. Pink
5. Green
6. Red
7. Yellow
8. Orange
9. Dark Red
10. Brown
11. Light Blue
12. Dark Green
13. Gold
14. Violet
15. Light Green

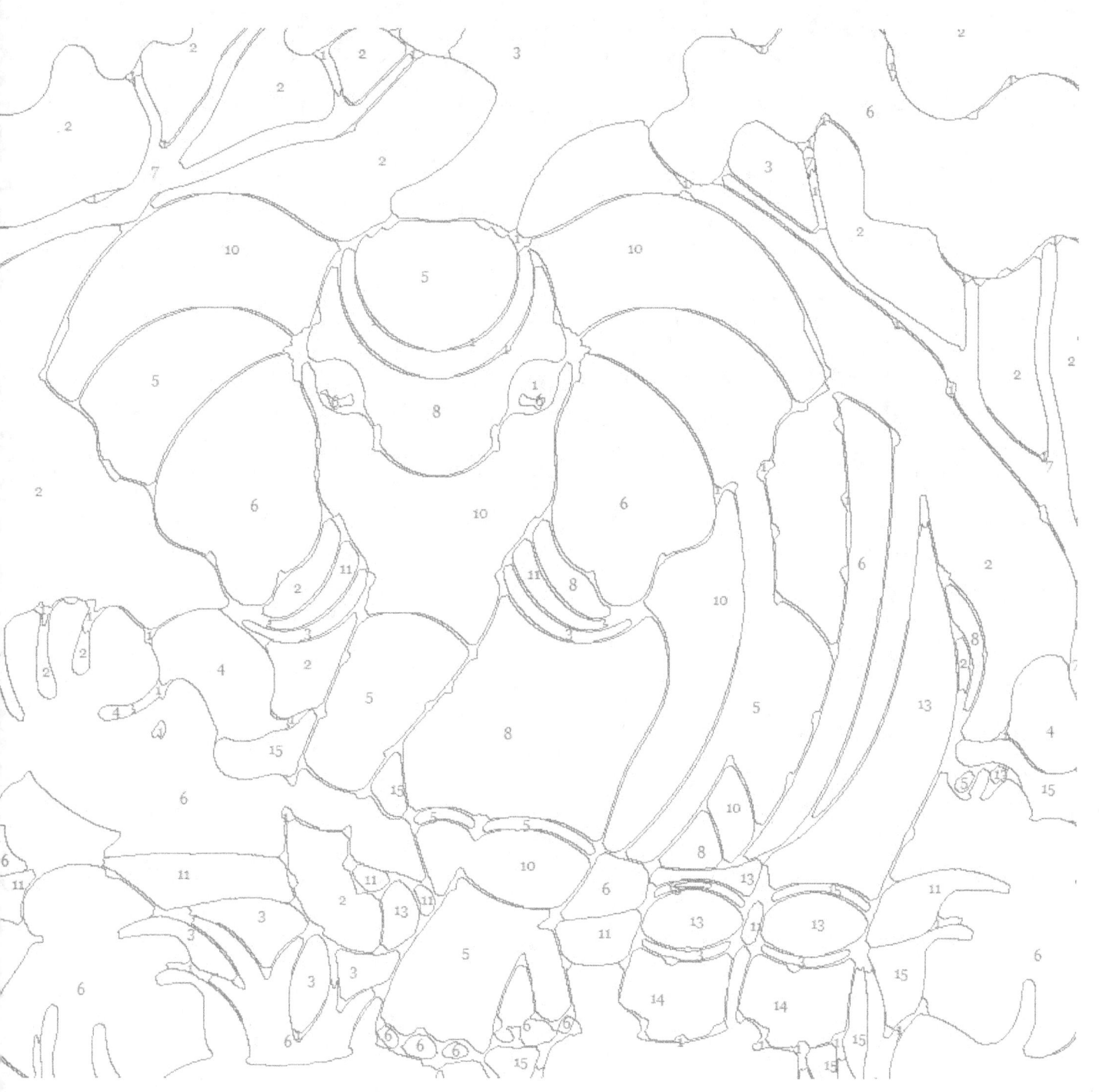

www.ingramcontent.com/pod-product-compliance
Lightning Source LLC
Chambersburg PA
CBHW082024230526
45466CB00023B/3361